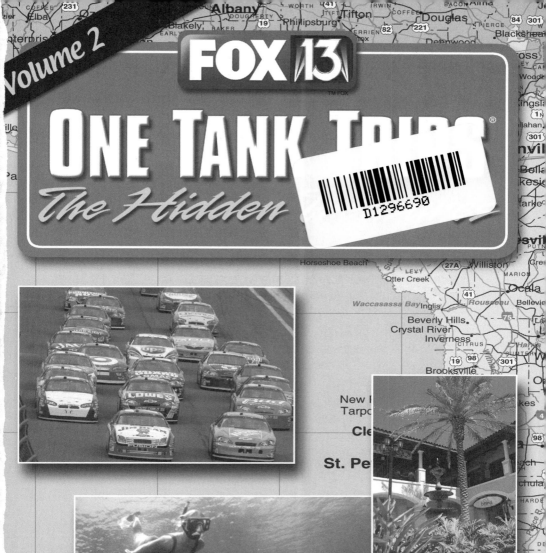

Volume 2

FOX 13

ONE TANK TRIPS®

The Hidden

Seaside
Publishing, Inc.

One Tank Trips® is a publication conceived and developed by WTVT FOX13 and published by Seaside Publishing Inc., a division of Famous Florida Enterprises, Inc.

PUBLISHER
Joyce LaFray - Seaside Publishing

PRODUCTION & DESIGN
Jim Wahl - FOX13
Kevin Coccaro - FOX13
Mo Eppley - Seaside Publishing

CONTRIBUTING WRITERS & EDITORS
Cary Williams - Image Criteria Group
Kelli Kwiatkowski - Seaside Publishing
FOX13 Staff

SEASIDE PUBLISHING STAFF
Patricia Mack - Senior Editor
Steven Groth - VP, Sales & Marketing

Additional copies of this book may be ordered by calling
1-888-ONE-TANK (663-8265)
Visit our Web site to order online at:
www.FoxOneTankTrips.com or **www.SeasidePublishing.com**
Or you may write Seaside Publishing at:
P.O. Box 14441, St. Petersburg, FL 33733

ISBN: 978-0-9760555-5-6
Library of Congress Catalog Number: 2008909892
© 2009 New World Communications of Tampa, Inc.

Photography - Front cover photo by Dan Gaye/Studio 75. 1963 Chevrolet Corvette Grand Sport courtesy of Ron & Linda Bauer/Speedpass Racing. Back cover clockwise left to right: Henry B. Plant Museum at University of Tampa (© University of Tampa); NASCAR at Daytona (© Daytona 500 Int.); Snorkler at John Pennekamp Coral Reef State Park (© Florida Parks Services); Courtyard at BayWalk (© BayWalk).
Interior photography - All photos copyright WTVT FOX13 unless indicated otherwise.
Title page photos - Top to bottom NASCAR at Daytona (© Daytona 500 Int.); Courtyard at BayWalk (© BayWalk); Snorkler at John Pennekamp Coral Reef State Park (© Florida Parks Services).

Special thanks to: Georgia Turner & Associates, Geiger & Associates, St. Petersburg/Clearwater CVB, Stuart Newman & Associates, Cindy Cockburn.

Special Sales: Bulk purchases (12+ copies) for FOX13 TAMPA BAY'S ONE TANK TRIPS® are available to companies at special discounts. For more information call Steven Groth, Vice President, Sales & Marketing at: 1-888-ONE-TANK (663-8265) or write to Seaside Publishing, Special Sales P.O. Box 14441, St. Petersburg, FL 33733.

While we have been very careful to assure the accuracy of the information in this guide, time brings change, and, consequently, the publisher cannot accept responsibility for discrepancies that may occur. All prices and hours of operation are based on information given to us at press time. These may change, so be sure to call ahead. We welcome comments, suggestions and tips for inclusion in future editions.

Acknowledgments

One Tank Trips® reflects the contributions of the dedicated staff at **FOX13**. This travel guide would not have been possible without the special efforts of:

Bill Schneider
Vice President & General Manager

Mike McClain
Vice President of News

Phil Metlin
Former Vice President of News

Mike House
Vice President of Creative Services

Jim Wahl
Design Director

Kevin Coccaro
Broadcast & Multimedia Designer

Carrie Schroeder
Promotion/Community Affairs Manager

A special thanks to:

Carolyn Forrest
Vice President, FTS

And every member of the FOX13 team

contents

contents

Florida map

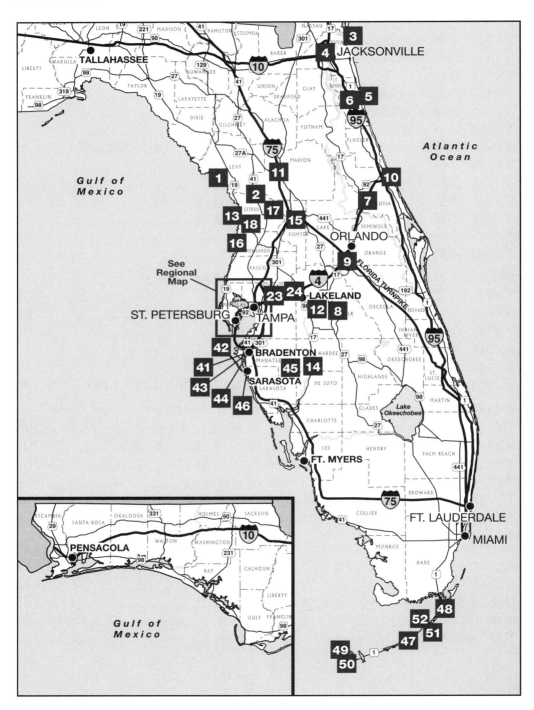

regional map

One Tank Trips

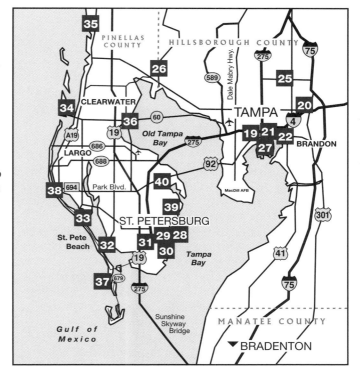

discover the **real** Florida

At **WTVT FOX13**, we enjoy taking viewers to off-the-beaten path travel spots. There is a good reason tourism is Florida's top industry. This picturesque state is populated with vibrant and interesting people. *One Tank Trips®: The Hidden Treasures* is designed to help you discover the best places and plan your own outings in the Tampa Bay area.

Whether you are headed to the colorful and historic town of Key West, or to paddle in cool clear water canoeing down the scenic Weeki Wachee River or to savor the fare at the century-old Columbia restaurant in Ybor City, you will want to have this handy guide at your side.

This unique travel book will satisfy anyone with an unrelenting wanderlust for discovering the real Florida. Packed with information for an enjoyable outing, *One Tank Trips®: The Hidden Treasures* contains travel tips and detailed maps. For quick access, keep it in your glove compartment. You will find it is a necessity!

"One Tank Trips®" is a proud part of the **WTVT FOX13** family and we know it will become a part of yours. So buckle up and enjoy 52 of Florida's best destinations, reachable on just one tank of gas.

a word from FOX13

Our first *One Tank Trips*® book was a huge success and quickly became a best seller in the state of Florida. The first publication was a result of the many calls we received each time one of our "**One Tank Trip®**" episodes aired. Our dedicated staff fielded numerous viewer requests for information, directions, phone numbers and admission prices. The book answered all of those queries and more. The overwhelming response made a second book inevitable. Now, *One Tank Trips®: The Hidden Treasures* satisfies the demand for even more excursions, highlighting 52 additional Florida destinations.

With great pride, all of us at **FOX13** are pleased to bring you *One Tank Trips®: The Hidden Treasures*. We've been busy putting a lot of miles behind us so you can enjoy more unique Florida destinations reachable on just one tank of gas.

Drive safely and be sure to watch **FOX13's "Good Day Tampa Bay"** for your next **"One Tank Trip®"**!

Bill Schneider

Bill Schneider
Vice President & General Manager
WTVT FOX13 Television

florida fairs

Florida's fantastic weather permits year-round celebrations at a variety of festivals and fairs. Here's a brief month-by-month calendar of just a few of the most popular events, many focused on historic traditions and foods indigenous to Florida. Visit the Web sites listed or call for specific information, dates and times to be sure that the event has not been rescheduled.

JANUARY
Annual Kiwanis Medieval Faire, Ft. Myers.
www.medieval-faire.com
(239)839-8036

Kumquat Festival, Dade City.
www.kumquatfestival.org
(352)567-3769

FEBRUARY
Florida State Fair, Tampa.
www.floridastatefair.com
(800)345-3247

Florida Strawberry Festival, Plant City.
www.flstrawberryfestival.com
(813)752-9194

Gasparilla Piratefest Invasion & Parade, Tampa.
www.gasparillapiratefest.com
(813)237-3258

South Beach Wine & Food Festival, Miami.
www.sobewineandfoodfest.com
(305)229-5249

MARCH
Annual Easter Boogie & World Record Dives, Zephyrhills.
www.mainstreetzephyrhills.org
(813)780-1414

Festival of States, St. Petersburg.
www.festivalofstates.com
(727)321-9888

Grant Seafood Festival, Grant.
www.grantseafoodfestival.com
(321)723-8687

Winter Park Sidewalk Art Festival, Winter Park.
www.wpsaf.org
(407)790-0597

APRIL
Cedar Key Arts Festival, Cedar Key.
www.cedarkeyartsfestival.com
(352)543-5400

Tampa Bay Blues Fest, St.Petersburg.
www.tampabaybluesfest.com
(727)502-5000

MAY
Blue Crab Festival, Downtown Palatka.
www.bluecrabfestival.com
(386)325-4406

Florida Folk Festival, White Springs.
www.floridafolkfestival.com
(877)635-3655

Ruskin Tomato & Heritage Festival, Ruskin.
www.ruskintomatofestival.org
(813)645-3808

Zellwood Sweet Corn Festival, Zellwood.
www.zellwoodcornfestival.com
(407)886-0014

and festivals

JUNE
Cuban American Heritage Festival, Key West.
www.cubanfest.com
(305)295-9665

Chiefland Watermelon Festival, Chiefland.
www.chieflandwatermelonfestival.com
(352)493-0911

JULY
International Mango Festival, Homestead.
www.fairchildgarden.org
(305)258-0464

AUGUST
Greek Winefest, Tarpon Springs.
www.spongedocks.net/tarpon-springs-events.htm
(813)629-8304

SEPTEMBER
Mid Florida Balloon Festival, Eustis.
www.midfloridaballoonfestival.com
(407)886-5393

Pensacola Seafood Festival, Pensacola.
www.visitpensacola.com
(850)432-1450

OCTOBER
Biketoberfest for motorcycling enthusiasts, Daytona Beach.
www.biketoberfest.org
(866)296-8970

John's Pass Seafood Festival, Madeira Beach.
www.johnspass.com
(727)397-9764

Cedar Key at the Birding & Wildlife Experience.
www.ncbwe.com
(352)543-5600

Fall Harvest & Peanut Festival, Williston.
www.willistonfl.com
(352)528-5552

San Antonio Rattlesnake Festival.
www.rattlesnakefestival.com
(352)588-4444

Stone Crab, Seafood & Wine Festival, Longboat Key.
www.colonybeachresort.com
(800) 4-COLONY

Swamp Buggy Races, Naples.
www.swampbuggy.com
(239)774-2701

NOVEMBER
Florida Seafood Festival, Apalachicola.
www.floridaseafoodfestival.com
(850)653-4720

Land O' Lakes Flapjack Festival.
www.centralpascochamber.com
(813)909-2722

Miami Book Fair International, Miami.
www.miamibookfair.com
(305)237-3258

Plant City Pig Jam, Plant City.
www.plantcitypigjam.com
(813)764-3707

Ribfest, St. Petersburg.
www.ribfest.org
(727)528-3828

DECEMBER
Miccosukee Indians Art Festival, Miami.
www.miccosukeeresort.com
(305)553-8365

Pioneer Florida Museum & Village Christmas Open House, Dade City.
www.pioneerfloridamuseum.org
(352)562-0262

FOX 13
ONE TANK TRIPS®
The Hidden Treasures

North Florida

The Village of Cedar Key

living on island time

The streets of downtown are lined with many historic homes, built with gables and porches, where residents preserve the island lifestyle.

the trip

Cedar Key is one of Florida's oldest ports and certainly one of the most beautiful. The peaceful setting is reminiscent of a time gone by. This lovely community has a unique appeal, attracting a multitude of artists and writers inspired by the pristine environment. The seafood you'll find here is abundant and superb!

what to see

Walk the historic streets, browse the shops and galleries, explore the back bayous and enjoy restaurants. The Island Room Restaurant which features fresh seafood from local waters is excellent. Have fun fishing, bird watching and hiking on nearby nature trails. Guides are also on call for off-shore trips to the outer islands. Many of these islands are part of the Cedar Key National Wildlife Refuge. Use the public marina for docking boats and other watercraft.

other highlights

Aquaculture is the cultivation of the waters' natural produce. It's a practice that flourishes here. Cedar Key's luscious clams are grown using new and faster methods. Thousands of visitors flock here for the annual Seafood Festival held in October, the Old Florida Celebration of the Arts in April and the Clamerica on the Fourth of July.

Cedar Key Area Chamber of Commerce
618 Second St.
Cedar Key, FL 32625
(352) 543-5600

Admission: *Free.*

Hours: *Restaurant and shop hours vary. Be sure to check ahead.*

www.cedarkey.org

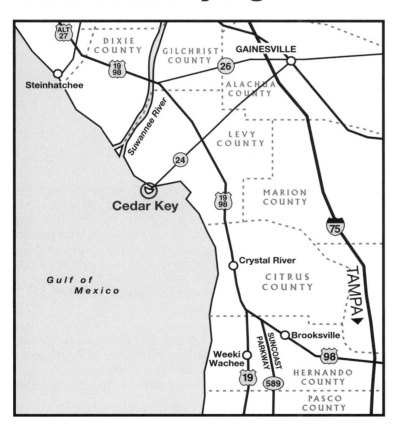

directions
From Tampa, take U.S. 19/98 north to State Road 24, about 100 miles. Travel southwest on S.R. 24 about 24 miles to the village of Cedar Key.

the 'key' to a fun day.

North Florida

Rainbow Springs State Park

making a splash

C. Revis

You are likely to see plenty of wildlife, like this cormorant, as you paddle your way down the Rainbow River.

the trip
Archaeologists say that people have been using Rainbow Springs for nearly 10,000 years. It is Florida's fourth largest natural spring and, from the 1930s through the 1970s, was the site of a popular, privately owned attraction. The Rainbow River is well-known for swimming, snorkeling, canoeing, and kayaking. Canoes and kayaks can be rented at two locations. Whether it is swimming or paddling in the cool water of the springs, picnicking in the park, hiking or birding along the nature or strolling through the gorgeous gardens, there are wonders to behold.

what to see
Take your pick of the six-mile-long, spring-fed Rainbow River or the beautiful Withlacoochee River. What a perfect setting to simply sit back, paddle when you like and enjoy. For non-swimmers, people with special needs and parents with small children, inflatable boats are available as well.

other highlights
You'll notice there are dragonflies everywhere. Not only are they exotic and amazing, their ancestors were around 100 million years before the dinosaurs! They are survivors, playing an important role in Florida's ecological chain. And despite their appearance, they do not sting and are quite harmless.

Rainbow Springs State Park
19158 S.W. 81st Place Rd.
Dunnellon, Florida 34432
(352) 465-8555

Tubing Entrance at 10830 SW 180th Avenue Road on the east side of the river.

Admission: *$1 per person, free for children younger than 6. Rentals for canoes, kayaks and tubes vary. Call for information.*

Hours: *8 a.m. until dusk.*
Rentals 10 a.m. to 6 p.m. daily.

Boat and tube rentals provided by:
Dragonfly Watersports
Canoe Dock at the Headsprings: (352) 465-2100

www.floridastateparks.org/rainbowsprings

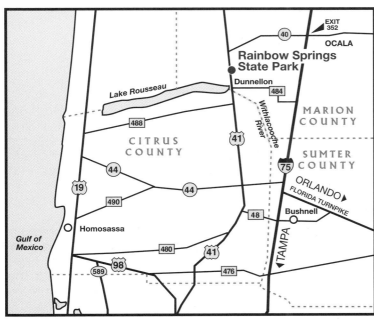

directions
From Tampa, take Interstate 75 to the second Ocala exit 352 onto State Road 40. Take S.R. 40 west until it dead-ends at U.S. 41. Turn left; the park entrance is on the left.

spend
an **hour**
or a day
on the
water.
It's **good**
for what
ails you.

North Florida

Kingsley Plantation

preserving the past

On the grounds are 23 slave quarters. One is restored to its original appearance.

Mike Booher

Zephaniah Kingsley and other plantation owners lived in this 1798 house.

the trip
Zephaniah Kingsley came to Spanish Florida in the early 19th century to make his fortune. He began by acquiring land and then building plantations using slave labor. Kingsley Plantation (originally Fort George Island) was established in 1814. It represents a unique time and place in Florida history. The stories and contributions of a people, free and enslaved, can be explored in the many exhibits.

what to see
Visitors can walk around the Kingsley's residence where he lived with his wife, Anna Madgigine Jai, and four children. Anna was a slave who Kingsley purchased and then freed. You will see the ruins of what once were 23 tabby (oyster shell and concrete) cabins and learn about the cultivation of plantation crops. Fields of Sea Island cotton, the primary crop of the plantation, once covered much of the island.

other highlights
It's believed the plantation's main residence dates back to 1798. It's an unusual structure, with a two-story central area and four square corner rooms. Today, the visitor center and historical exhibits are located in the Historic Fort George Lodge.

Kingsley Plantation
11676 Palmetto Avenue
Jacksonville, FL 32226
(904) 251-3537

Admission: *Free.*

Hours: *Daily 9 a.m. to 5 p.m.*
Closed Thanksgiving, Christmas Day and New Year's Day.

**www.nps.gov/history/nr/travel/
geo-flor/21.htm**

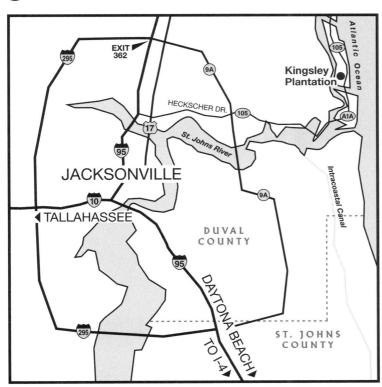

directions

From Tampa, take Interstate 4 north, merge onto Interstate 95 towards Jacksonville. Take exit 362 east to Heckscher Drive. Heckscher Drive becomes A1A. Head east about 15 miles. Take a left onto Fort George Road, then another left onto Palmetto Avenue to Kingsley Plantation, about 2 miles.

at **Kingsley** Plantation, the **stories** will be **told** forever.

The Ritz Theatre & LaVilla Museum

puttin' on the Ritz

An entire exhibit in the LaVilla Museum is dedicated to James Weldon Johnson, a LaVilla native.

The Ritz Theatre and LaVilla Museum

The restored Ritz Theatre is host to a variety of arts.

the trip

The famous Ritz Theatre, which opened in 1929, has been lovingly reconstructed. The structure shines as it did when LaVilla, a Jacksonville neighborhood, earned the nickname "the Harlem of the South." Enjoy browsing through the 32,000-square-foot museum and theater. It features exhibits focusing on the history of African-American life in LaVilla and Northeast Florida.

what to see

The mission of the 11,000-square-foot museum is to discover, preserve, and share historical and cultural African-American experiences. The 400-seat theater plays host to weddings, national recording artists, touring productions and gospel shows. A must-see is the exhibit dedicated to James Weldon Johnson. The LaVilla native wrote the remarkable "Lift Every Voice and Sing." First a poem, then a song, it came to be known as the African-American national anthem.

other highlights

The museum will tell you the complete story of LaVilla, the good and bad, the inspirational and regrettable. Experience the neighborhood drugstore the way it used to be, along with other historic sections of the community. A part of the story is unique to Jacksonville, while another is a reflection of national changes.

Ritz Theatre & LaVilla Museum
829 N. Davis Street
Jacksonville, FL 32202
(904) 632-5555

Admission: *Museum $6 adults, $3 students and seniors. Theater prices vary.*

Hours: *Tuesday through Friday 10 a.m. to 6 p.m., Saturday 10 a.m. to 2 p.m., Sunday 2 p.m. to 5 p.m. Theater hours vary.*

www.ritzlavilla.org

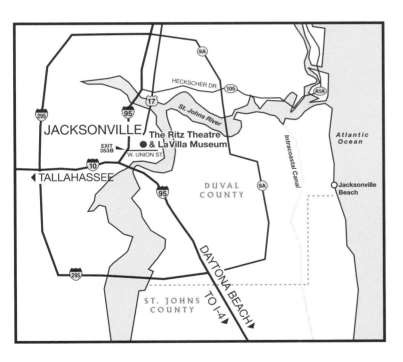

directions

From Tampa, take Interstate 4, merge onto Interstate 95 north towards Jacksonville. Take exit 353-B (Union Street) towards the sports complex and riverfront. Merge onto West Union Street and follow about 400 feet to North Davis Street. Turn left and you will be at The Ritz Theatre and LaVilla Museum.

once **known** as the **'Harlem** of the South,' there is a **wonderful** rebirth underway **in this** neighborhood.

North Florida

St. Augustine & Castillo de San Marcos

history and "magic" at every turn

In St. Augustine, situated at the mouth of two rivers on the Atlantic, history endures at every turn.

St. Johns County VCB

the trip

Founded in 1565, St. Augustine is the oldest continuously occupied European settlement in the United States. The city is filled with much to see and do. Be ready to spend some time in this historic community.

what to see

You will want to bring your camera when you visit here! More than 80 historic sites and attractions await. A must-see is the romantic, historic Castillo de San Marcos on Matanzas Bay. It's the oldest masonry fort in the continental United States. Just to the south is the elegant Bridge of Lions. Nearby is historic St. George Street which is the city's "outdoor mall," where you will find a huge collection of gift shops and restaurants. One of the most memorable stops is the Lightner Museum with its unusual furniture and a ballroom that was once the world's largest pool!

other highlights

Be sure to visit the Fountain of Youth. According to tradition, Ponce de Leon discovered this magical spring after he landed in St. Augustine on April 2, 1513. Enjoy Osteen's Restaurant for fresh shrimp!

St. Augustine Visitors Bureau
88 Riberia Street, Suite 400
St. Augustine, FL 32084
(904) 829-6506
Toll free: (800) 653-2489
Castillo de San Marcos
One South Castillo Drive
St. Augustine, FL 32084

Admission: *Free. The Castillo de San Marcos is free for children 15 and younger. Children must be accompanied by an adult, $6 for adults, $50 for wedding permits.*

Hours: *Restaurant, shop, museum and attraction hours vary. Castillo is open 8:45 a.m. to 4:45 p.m. daily, except December 25th.*

www.oldcity.com

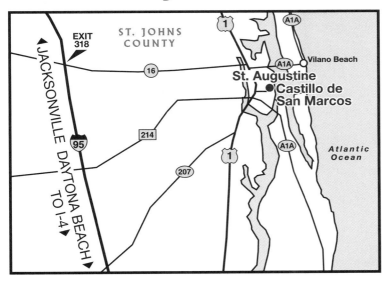

directions

From Tampa, take Interstate 4 north to Interstate 95. Take the St. Augustine Historic Sites and Downtown exit 318 (State Road 16) to U.S. 1. Head south on U.S. 1 for about two miles to One Castillo Drive. Parking is ahead on the left. Castillo de San Marcos is located in downtown St. Augustine.

the sightseeing is nothing short of spectacular.

North Florida

San Sebastian Winery

a wine for every taste

The handsome San Sebastian Winery building attracts visitors who want to sample a little history with their wine.

the trip

Welcome to San Sebastian! Tucked away in a corner of historic St. Augustine, you will find the San Sebastian Winery. It's one of only a handful of wineries in all of Florida. This handsome structure is located on the San Sebastian River. It's part of a complex designed by Henry Flagler to house the historic East Coast Railway. These days, the focus is on the production of delicious wines.

what to see

The barrel room of course! In the intimate setting you'll find wine for nearly every palate, including San Sebastian Reserve, Chablis, Vintners White and Red, Port, and Cream Sherry. The adventurous owners have entered many major competitions. Numerous awards are an indication of the success of their winemaking techniques. Wine tours operate daily.

other highlights

The gourmet gift shop offers many wine and food related items. There's live music on weekends weather permitting, tastings and a special picnic area.

San Sebastian Winery
157 King Street
St. Augustine, FL 32084
Toll free: (888) 352-9463
(904) 826-1594

Admission: *Free.*

Hours: *Individuals and groups are welcome Monday through Saturday 10 a.m. to 6 p.m., Sunday 11 a.m. to 6 p.m.*

www.sansebastianwinery.com

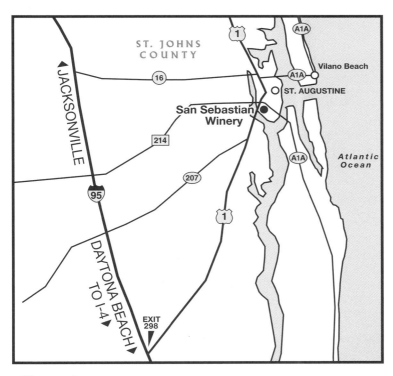

directions

From Tampa, take Interstate 4 east to Interstate 95. Go north (towards Jacksonville) on Interstate 95 to exit 298 (U.S. 1/A1A) towards St. Augustine. Follow U.S. 1 about 16 miles, then turn right onto King Street. San Sebastian is about 100 yards on your right.

make **this** part of **your** St. Augustine experience.

Central Florida

Cassadaga Spiritualist Camp

communicating with spirit

Visitors are welcomed to the spiritualist camp that was founded in 1894. Healing services are held at the Colby Temple.

the trip

You will marvel at the quaint beauty of the 57-acre Cassadaga Spiritualist Camp. It's the oldest, active religious community in the Southeastern United States and was designated a Historic District on the National Register of Historic Places in 1991. The camp was founded by George P. Colby in 1894. Mr. Colby lived in New York, but he dreamed of a place in the South where his religion and spiritualism could be shared.

what to see

There are approximately 100 people who reside within the Cassadaga Spiritualist Camp. About half are practicing psychics or certified mediums available for readings and consultations. Residents may own their homes, but the Camp retains ownership of the land. Sunday morning church services include hymns, a guided meditation, healing, a lecture, musical interludes and messages brought by a certified medium.

other highlights

It's important to distinguish between the town of Cassadaga and the Camp. Many businesses offer an array of religious and psychic readings, such as Tarot, palm divination and crystal ball gazing. Most are located around the perimeter of the Camp. The Camp does not invalidate these sciences when performed by experienced practitioners, but they are not carried out on campgrounds. The camp offers Wednesday night readings by certified mediums from 7:30 p.m. to 9 p.m. A $5 donation is requested.

The Cassadaga Hotel
& Psychic Center
355 Cassadaga Road
Cassadaga, FL 32706
(386) 228-2323

Admission: *Free. Rates vary at the hotel. Reservations are highly recommended.*

www.cassadagahotel.net

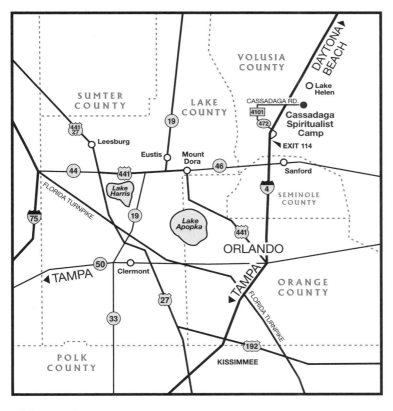

directions

From Tampa, take Interstate 4 north to exit 114 (State Road 472) towards Orange City/Deland. Stay on S.R. 472 west. Make a right onto Dr. Martin Luther King, Jr. Beltway. Turn right onto Cassadaga Road. The Cassadaga Hotel will be on the right-hand side where the road curves to the left into Lake Helen.

regardless **of** how you **feel** about psychics, Cassadaga **is** an **enchanting** destination.

Chalet Suzanne Inn & Restaurant

an enchanting Old World tradition

Swiss-costumed waitresses pamper guests with the Chalet's famous Southern hospitality.

Chalet Suzanne

The Balcony Honeymoon Room offers a luxurious, round bed and private dining balcony.

the trip

There is some magnificent magic going on at this European-style village. The Chalet's setting is lovely. It's surrounded by an orange grove in its own National Historic District. Four generations of the Hinshaw family have lived and worked at this 70-acre country inn.

what to see

The Chalet has several gourmet dining rooms. A bridal suite overlooks one of them, with a dumbwaiter to deliver your meals. That way, you never have to leave. The Chalet's soup is world famous. As a matter of fact, it's out of this world — literally. This signature recipe, "Soup Romaine," is also called "Moon Soup." It was served as a special freeze-dried delicacy on flights of Apollo 15, 16 and Apollo-Soyuz.

other highlights

Stop by the autograph garden. It's a relaxing setting and the site of many weddings. You can design your own "love" plaque at the ceramic shop and add it to others in the garden. There's also History House, the Chalet's museum, a gift shop, wine shop, a library and a gourmet soup cannery where the Chalet's famous soups are processed and then sold around the world. By the way, if you don't want to drive here, then fly. Chalet Suzanne has its own airstrip! Just let them know when you're coming.

Chalet Suzanne Inn & Restaurant
3800 Chalet Suzanne Drive
Lake Wales, FL 33859
Toll free: (800) 433-6011
(863) 676-6011

Admission: *You are free to walk around the grounds and visit the restaurant and shops. Room rates vary from $169 to $229; special rates out of season. A stay includes a luscious country breakfast. Restaurant: Four-course lunches begin at $29; six-course candlelit dinner begins at $59; a la carte menu is available for all meals.*

Hours: *Open year round.*

www.ChaletSuzanne.com

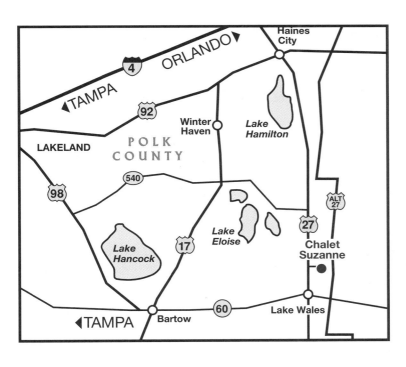

directions
From Tampa, take State Road 60 east to Lake Wales. Exit onto U.S. 27 north; go four miles. Turn right onto Chalet Suzanne Road.

a **taste** of a **Florida favorite.**

TRIP **9**

Central Florida

Gatorland

alligators abound

Gatorland

Oblivious to piggy-backing birds, thousands of gators enjoy their Gatorland home.

the trip

Set aside at least half a day to spend at this 110-acre park and wildlife preserve — long considered the "Alligator Capital of the World." It has one of the world's largest exhibits of giant gators. You'll also see free-flying lorikeets (Australian parrots), pink flamingos and a whole lot more!

what to see

The Gator Jumparoo show has made this attraction world-famous. You will be amazed as dozens of gators, some as long as 13 feet, leap out of the water and perform for their supper. And check out the gator wrestling, where the craziest of daredevils step into the ring to tangle with one of these fearless reptiles. It's man versus beast and quite a sight to behold!

other highlights

Photographers from around the world journey to this 10-acre bird sanctuary. The refuge is home to many rare, endangered and protected species of birds. The preserve offers birdwatchers a unique opportunity to get up close and personal on an elevated walkway that winds through the alligator breeding marsh.

Gatorland
14501 S. Orange Blossom Trail
Orlando, FL 32837
Toll free: (800) 393-JAWS (5297)
(407) 855-5496

Admission: *$22.95 adults, $14.95 children 3 to 12, free for children 2 and younger.*

Hours: *Daily 9 a.m., closing times vary with the season.*

www.gatorland.com

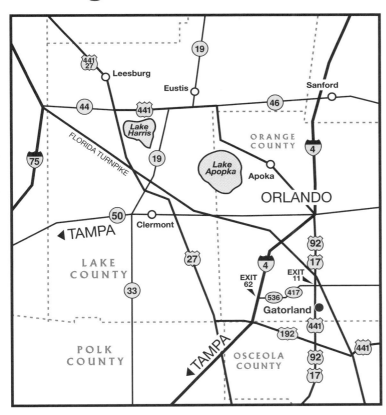

directions

From Tampa, take Interstate 4 east to exit 62. Take State Road 417 (The Greenway, a toll road). Take exit 11 for Orange Blossom Trail (S.R. 441). Bear right onto Orange Blossom Trail (S.R. 441); head south approximately 1 mile. Gatorland is on the left.

see you
later...

Central Florida

Daytona 500 Experience

magical motor sports memories

International Speedway Corporation.

The IMAX® 3-D movie theater brings racing action to larger-than-life. Thousands of visitors have enjoyed an inside and exciting glimpse of racing history at the Daytona 500.

the trip

Open since 1996, this interactive family motor sports attraction celebrates the history of racing in Daytona Beach since the early 1900s.

what to see

Share the thrill of racing in simulators during track tours and at the IMAX® 3D movie theater. Test your pit crew potential at the "Chevy 16-Second Pit Stop Challenge." Goodyear Heritage of Daytona history walk takes guests back through time, allowing them the opportunity to see how Daytona came to be a world center for racing.

other highlights

See NASCAR's "Car Of Tomorrow" and the winning Daytona 500 car. Browse the Pit Shop, the large souvenir and apparel store and savor a burger at the Fourth Turn Grill. Plan to spend a good part of your day here at this remarkable and historical attraction.

Daytona International Speedway
1801 W. International Speedway Blvd.
Daytona Beach, FL 32114
(386) 947-6800

Admission: *$24 adults, $19 seniors and children (6 to 12), free for children younger than 5.*

Hours: *Daily 9 a.m. to 7 p.m. (Subject to change during special events).*

www.daytona500experience.com

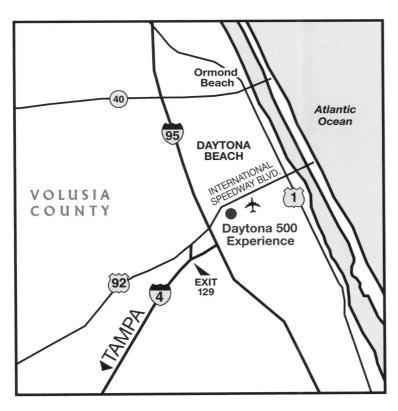

directions

From Tampa, take Interstate 4 to exit 129 then head east onto U.S. 92 (International Speedway Blvd.). Continue east on International Speedway Blvd. (U.S. 92) for about 1 mile. Daytona 500 Experience's entrance will be on your right side at NASCAR Drive.

Don Garlits Museum of Drag Racing

Big Daddy's on the fast track

Don Garlits Museum of Drag Racing

More than 175 collectable, antique, and specialty race cars are on display at this mecca for automotive fans. The classic trailer and car are not just museum pieces, but a tribute to Don Garlits and his love of auto racing.

the trip

"Big Daddy" as the late Don Garlits was known, opened two museums here — the Museum of Drag Racing and the Museum of Classic Automobiles. Your admission ticket is valid for both.

what to see

You don't have to be a dragster to appreciate the colorful displays of racing cars and racing memorabilia that chronicle more than fifty years of drag racing history. The home-built hot rods from back in the day with their multiple carburetors are incredible. So are the sleek tubular chassis and the supercharged engines that burn nitromethane fuel of the modern age. And don't miss the U.S. Navy A-7 Corsair Attack Fighter poised for flight. Superstar Garlits took great pleasure in putting this all together.

other highlights

Take a look at the 1956 Chrysler Imperial that once belonged to former President Dwight D. Eisenhower. The impeccably kept and maintained vehicle at the Museum of Classic Automobiles was specially made for the president as a birthday present from First Lady Mamie.

Don Garlits
Museum of Drag Racing
13700 SW 16th Ave.
Ocala, FL 34473
(352) 245-8661
Toll free: (877) 271-3278

Admission: *$15 adults, $13 students and seniors 60 and older, $6 children 5 to 12, free for children younger than 5.*

Hours: *Daily 9 a.m. to 5 p.m. Closed Christmas.*

www.garlits.com

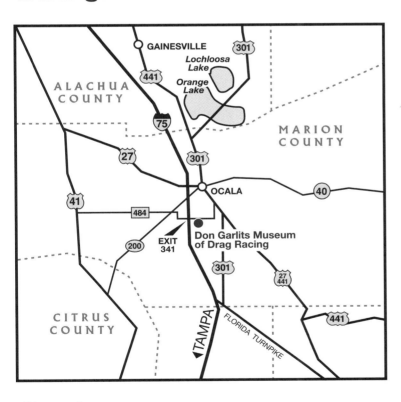

directions
From Tampa, take Interstate 75 to exit 341, toward Belleview/Dunnellon. Take County Road 484 east toward Belleview. Turn right onto Southwest 16th Avenue.

an exciting
experience
in
innovation
and evolution.

Polk County Historical Museum

a valuable link to the past

Polk County Historical Museum

The fascinating military exhibit is one of many inside the Polk County Historical Museum where extensive renovations have breathed new life into the Polk County Courthouse.

the trip

The historic Polk County Courthouse in Bartow is impressive and really quite stunning. Built in 1908, the courthouse is now home to the Polk County Historical Museum, where the standing invitation is "take a trip into the past."

what to see

You will find newspaper clippings, photos and fascinating information about old Polk County. Some of the antique bottles on display are more than 120 years old. There is also an impressive collection of arrowheads, all found in Polk County.

other highlights

The Polk County Historical and Genealogical Library is located in the east wing of the Historic Courthouse. It was first opened to the public in January of 1940. It boasts one of the largest genealogical and historical collections in the Southeast United States.

Polk County Historical Museum
100 E. Main Street
Bartow, FL 33830
(863) 534-4386

Admission: *Free.*

Hours: *Tuesday through Friday 9 a.m. to 5 p.m., Saturday 9 a.m. to 3 p.m.*

www.polkcountymuseum.org

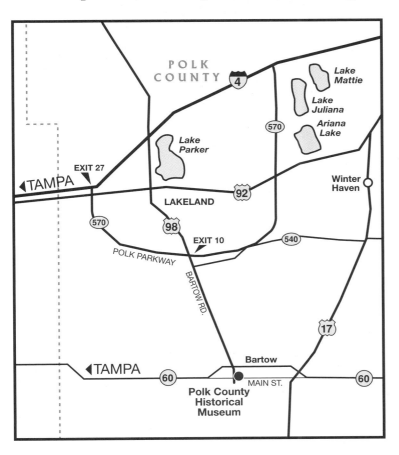

directions

From Tampa, take Interstate 4 to exit 27 (State Road 570 east). Take exit 10 (U.S. 98) to Bartow Road. Follow U.S. 98 south to Main Street. The museum is near the intersection of Main Street and North Broadway.

beautifully **restored,** this **little** **museum** really **shines.**

Central Florida

River Safaris & Gulf Charters

explore the beauty of the Nature Coast

River Safaris & Gulf Charters

A tour down the lazy Homosassa River is a relaxing experience. Manatees welcome visitors during the winter months.

the trip

Many adventures await you at this mom-and-pop boat tour and rental facility on the beautiful Homosassa River. The owners, Captain Dennis Lowe and his wife Alicia, feel strongly about getting people out on the river to learn its history and to see this ballet of nature firsthand.

what to see

Ah, the river! There are several pontoon tours available. A combination spring and backwater tour meanders past Monkey Island, home to five spider monkeys. You will also see a gazebo, once a favorite spot of President Grover Cleveland. The former Commander-In-Chief lived in Homosassa and could be seen fishing on warm summer evenings. Be sure to spend a little time in the remarkable gallery where the work of local artists is featured. The gift shop is a party for the eyes, with fun aquatic items everywhere.

other highlights

Another way to experience the tropical beauty of the Homosassa River is to jump right in! During the winter months you can swim with the manatees.

River Safaris & Gulf Charters
10823 Yulee Drive
Homosassa, FL 34448
Toll free: (800) 758-3474
(352) 628-5222

Rates: Boat tours from $18 per person for spring and backwater tours to $39 for the long backwater and springs-to-Gulf trips. All-day boat rentals $140 for a 18-to-20-foot; $160 for a 21-foot boat; $225 for a 25-foot pontoon. Note: Rentals are higher during scallop season.

Hours: Daily 8 a.m. to 5 p.m. Tours depart at 9 a.m., 11 a.m., 1 p.m., 3 p.m., and 5 p.m.

www.riversafaris.com

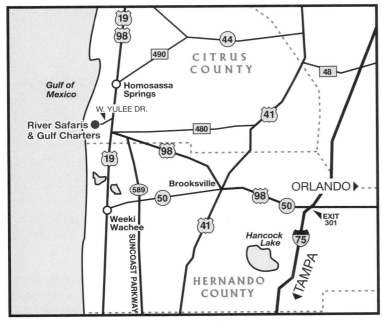

directions

From Tampa, take Interstate 75 to exit 301 onto U.S. 98 west towards Brooksville. Turn right (north) on U.S. 19 and proceed about 4 to 5 miles. Turn left onto West Yulee Drive and continue for 2 miles, heading west. Turn left onto Yulee Drive. River Safaris & Gulf Charters are located about 1 mile on the right.

the **beauty**
and **serenity**
of **this** river
will **soothe**
your
soul.

Solomon's Castle

his home really is his castle!

Solomon's Castle

It's a pleasant surprise to find Solomon's Castle and The Boat in the Moat restaurant seemingly in the middle of nowhere.

the trip

Three decades ago, an internationally known sculptor and host extraordinare settled near Ona and built a castle with his own hands. Be assured: If some people walk to the beat of a different drummer, then Howard Solomon has an entire symphony orchestra, with extra percussion!

what to see

There's lots of unique (to say the least) and amazing stuff to see here. The castle's exterior is big and shiny. It glistens and happens to be made from newspaper printing plates. Outside you will see a tower and more than 80 interpretive stained glass windows. Inside are extensive galleries, a stained-glass production studio and the family's living quarters. And there's "The Blue Moon Room," a spacious suite available for overnight or weekend stays.

other highlights

While out in this middle-of-nowhere location, take advantage of the miles of beautiful nature trails around picturesque Horse Creek.

Solomon's Castle
4533 Solomon Road
Ona, FL 33865
(863) 494-6077

Admission: *$10 adults, $4 children.*

Hours: *Tuesday through Sunday 11 a.m. to 4 p.m. Closed July, August and September.*

www.solomonscastle.com

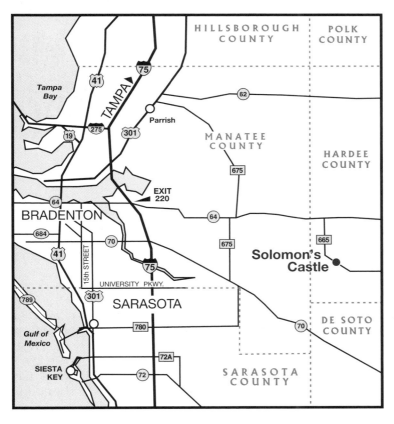

directions

From Tampa, take Interstate 75 south to exit 220 (State Road 64, Bradenton/Wauchula/Zolfo Springs). Turn left on S.R. 64 and go east about 30 miles to County Road 665. Turn right on C.R. 665 and go south for about nine miles. Take a hard left onto Solomon Road and follow less than a mile to Solomon's Castle.

a man's **home** is his **castle**, and yours, **too.**

Webster Flea Markets

Florida's attic

There is a lot of activity and plenty of goodies to choose from every Monday, flea market day in Webster.

Webster Westside Flea Market

Central Florida

the trip

Ready to do some serious shopping? Well, Florida has some flea markets for you! The Webster Flea Markets are among the oldest in the state. Add in the Sumter County Farmer's Market across the street along with two smaller markets and you'll have quite a day!

what to see

Here you will find an absolutely remarkable and enormous mix of people and stuff — LOTS of stuff and LOTS of people — but only on Mondays. The Monday thing started during the Depression. Local farmers, facing tough times, organized a farmers co-op. The "blue law" kept them from doing business on Sundays. So hello Monday! On some days, there are as many as 4,000 dealers and 100,000 shoppers.

other highlights

The Sumter County Farmer's Market, across from Webster Westside is the largest. This market attracts about 1,200 dealers in the summer and 2,000 during the winter. It features antiques, jewelry, furniture, fresh produce, plants, citrus trees and more. As for eats, there are plenty of concession stands everywhere. The first Monday of each month there is a classic car and motorcycle show from 8 a.m. to 3 p.m. The cost is $3 for adults; children 14 and younger are free.

Webster Westside Flea Market
516 N.W. Third Street
Webster, FL 33597
Toll free: (800) 832-7396
(352) 793-9877 (Monday only)

Sumter County Farmer's Market
524 N. Market Boulevard
Highway 471
Webster, FL 33597
(352) 793-2021

Admission: *Free. Parking costs about $3.*

Hours: *Mondays 6 a.m. to 3 p.m.*
Closed on federal holidays.

www.websterfleamarket.net

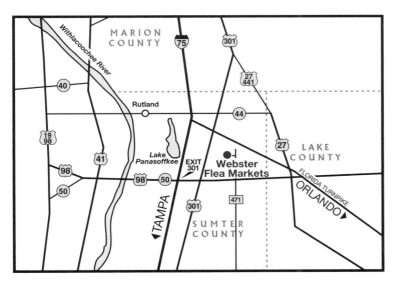

directions

From Tampa, take Interstate 75 north to exit 301 (State Road 50). Keep left at the fork to go on S.R. 50 east. Turn left onto S.R. 471. Turn left onto N.W. Fourth Avenue (County Road 478). Turn right onto North West Third Street.

Central Florida

Weeki Wachee Canoe & Kayak Rental

paddle your troubles away

The natural beauty of the river surrounds you at Rogers Park. Whether you wade in or swing from a rope Tarzan-style, be sure to take advantage of the crystal clear Weeki Wachee waters.

Weeki Wachee Canoe Rental

the trip

Encounter the beauty of the crystal clear Weeki Wachee River from a canoe or kayak. Normally, the current is not strong and paddling is fairly easy. When you reach the end of your seven-mile journey, transportation will be waiting for the short drive back to where you began.

what to see

Along the trip, expect to see plenty of wildlife, including manatees, turtles and birds. Once you are past the large "Wildlife Preserve" sign (about 20-30 minutes from the ramp) you can also go swimming or fishing.

other highlights

After your visit, spend some time at Weeki Wachee Springs. It's one of Florida's oldest theme parks and home to those famous, beautiful mermaids. Weeki Wachee is featured in our first "**One Tank Trips®**" book, *Fun Florida Adventures*.

Weeki Wachee Canoe & Kayak Rental
6131 Commercial Way
Spring Hill, FL 34606
(352) 597-0360
(352) 596-2628 Information Line

Admission: *$52 per two-seat canoe, $37 per single-seat kayak. Includes seat backs, life jackets, paddles and the return ride upstream.*

Hours: *Call for launch and pick-up times since they vary seasonally.*

www.floridacanoe.com

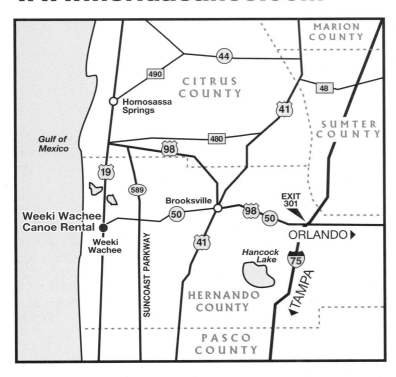

directions
From Tampa, take Veterans Expressway which turns into Suncoast Parkway north to State Road 50 (U.S. 98 west) to U.S. 19. Weeki Wachee is at the intersection of U.S. 19 and S.R. 50.

It **takes** about two seconds **to** **realize** this is going to **be** a **memorable** ride.

Central Florida

Withlacoochee State Trail

nature-lovers utopia

The trail's smooth, paved roads — combined with good company and beautiful scenery — make for a fun, healthy excursion.

Judith Watson

the trip

The trail is a paved 46-mile long, 12-foot wide stretch of old railroad bed that's been converted into a recreational area. The World Wildlife Fund calls it one of the "10 Coolest Places i North America." It's great for cycling, in-line skating, hiking and horseback riding.

what to see

From one end of Citrus County to the other, extending into Hernando and parts of Pasco, the trail meanders through some of the wildest, most beautiful scenery in all of Florida. Much of the trail passes through the Withlacoochee State Forest. It is the second largest state forest in Florida, covering more than 154,000 acres. There are several waterways and many varieties of trees. All combine to create dense woodlands and canopy trails. An abundance of colorful wildflowers excite the senses, especially in the spring.

other highlights

A portion of the trail includes Fort Cooper, a temporary fortification established in 1836 during the Second Seminole War. At certain times of the year, mainly in the fall and winter, the forest surrounding the trail becomes a hunting area. Fishing is also a popular activity on the Withlacoochee waterways. Panfish and largemouth bass are frequently caught here.

Withlacoochee State Trail
315 North Apopka Avenue
Inverness, FL 34450
(352) 726-2251

Admission: *Free.*

Hours: *Daily, sunrise to sundown.*

www.floridagreenwaysandtrails.com

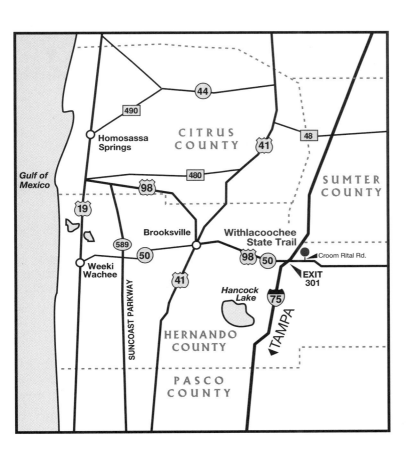

directions
From Tampa, take Interstate 75 to exit 301 for U.S. 98/50. Head east about 1 mile to Croom Rital Road. Take a left and proceed to trailhead.

miles and miles of happy trails!

Chassahowitzka River Wildlife Tours

eco-tourism at its best

Central Florida

A bird lover's delight, Chassahowitzka is home to herons, grackles and a wide variety of other birds. Touring the Chassahowitzka River on a slow-moving pontoon is the leisurely way to enjoy the sights and sounds of nature.

Ken Luther

the trip

Just south of Homosassa lies a serene and tranquil slice of true Florida beauty: the Chassahowitzka (say "Chas-ah-hoe-wit-ska") River. In the Seminole Indian language, Chassahowitzka means "place of hanging pumpkin." It is a feast for the eyes in any language. Captain Ken Luther, owner of Chassahowitzka River Wildlife Tours, is a wealth of information when it comes to the area. He shares that knowledge freely and with great joy during his pontoon tours.

what to see

The Chassahowitzka National Wildlife Refuge covers more than 30,000 acres. The trip begins in the river's spring-fed fresh water. The shore is dotted with cypress, oaks, cedars, sweet gum and a variety of other trees. With the salty waters of the Gulf of Mexico ahead, you may catch sight of deer, black bears, raccoons or perhaps a bobcat.

other highlights

The river is home to many fish, dolphins, gators and even manatee. Bird-lovers should bring binoculars for a glimpse of Louisiana herons, yellow-crowned night herons, boat-tailed grackles and other feathered friends. Bring sunscreen and hats, along with a picnic lunch to enjoy during your quick stop on "Dog Island."

Chassahowitzka River Wildlife Tours
8215 West Bounty Court
Homosassa, FL 34448
(352) 382-0837

Admission: *Rates vary. Call for information.*

Hours: *Tours by appointment. Parking fee $2.*

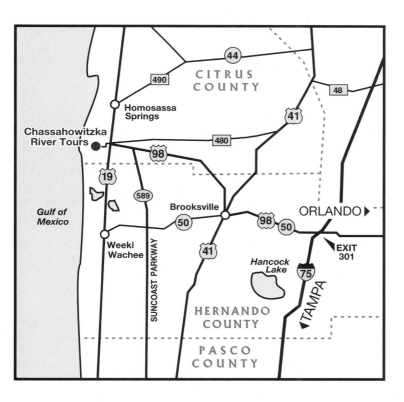

directions

From Tampa, take Veterans Expressway north which turns into Suncoast Parkway. Turn left on State Road 98 and continue across US 19, after which S.R. 98 becomes Miss Maggie Drive/County Road 480 west. Follow the yellow line until it ends. Turn right onto Chassahowitzka River Campground. Continue 1/4 mile to boat the ramp.

ecotourism at its beautiful best.

Henry B. Plant Museum

quintessential Victoriana

Hillsborough County – West Central Florida

Housed within the splendid Moorish building, the Henry B. Plant Museum displays opulent furnishings, and spectacular tropical gardens that were the crowning glory of Plant's Tampa Bay Hotel.

the trip

This Victorian architectural icon has been a Tampa landmark for more than 100 years. Built by railroad entrepreneur Henry Bradley Plant, this once grand resort is now a museum to the Gilded Age.

what to see

Take a step back in time as you view the museum's exhibits of how the wealthy spent their leisure time in the late 1800s. Explore the opulent rambling verandas, horseshoe arches, minarets and cupolas — all hallmarks of extraordinary Turkish and Moorish fantasy architecture. Don't miss a visit to the Spinning Girl — a life-sized sculpture made of cast iron and finished with a bronze patina. She adorned the lobby to welcome guests as they departed their private rail cars and entered the grand hotel. Today she stands before a rare 12-foot painted tapestry.

other highlights

Special exhibits in the Spanish-American War Room detail the hotel's role in the 1898 war when Tampa was the closest port to Spanish-held Cuba.

Henry B. Plant Museum
401 W. Kennedy Blvd.
Tampa, FL 33606
(813) 254-1891

Admission: *A donation of $5 for adults and $2 for children younger than 12 is requested January through November.*

Hours: *The Museum and Museum Store are open Tuesday through Saturday, 10 a.m. to 4 p.m. and Sunday, noon to 4 p.m. Closed Mondays (January to November), Thanksgiving Day, Christmas Eve and Christmas Day.*

www.plantmuseum.com

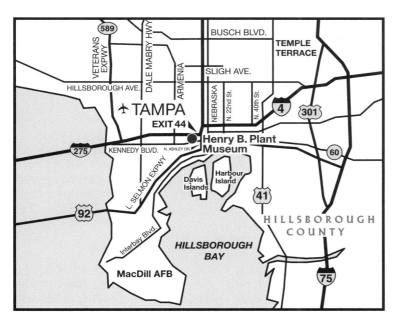

directions

From Interstate 275 south, take exit 45A to Downtown West, Ashley Drive. Proceed to Kennedy Boulevard, turn right, cross bridge, and drive 1/4 mile to The University of Tampa on your right. From Interstate 275 north, take exit 44, Ashley Drive, and proceed to Kennedy Boulevard. Turn right on Kennedy Boulevard, cross the bridge. The museum is located 1/4 mile on the right.

turn **back** time to a **more** elegant era. **Waltz,** anyone?

Seminole Hard Rock Hotel & Casino

get into the game

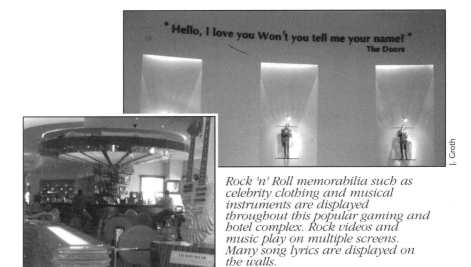

"Hello, I love you Won't you tell me your name?"
The Doors

J. Groth

Rock 'n' Roll memorabilia such as celebrity clothing and musical instruments are displayed throughout this popular gaming and hotel complex. Rock videos and music play on multiple screens. Many song lyrics are displayed on the walls.

the trip

Owned by Florida's indigenous Seminole Tribe, this casino has game. Count among the amenities a spacious non-smoking poker room. Not into gambling? Enjoy live music at the cozy lobby bar or savor the Fresh Harvest Buffet that serves specialties such as dim sum and steamed crab legs. Sample sizzling steaks and polished service at the Council Oak Steak House or fancy Floyd's.

what to see

Recently the Tribe built a two-story, 150,000-square-foot addition to house another 1,100 gaming machines, which brings the total now to 3,180. Music memorabilia abounds — there's a Jimi Hendrix jacket, James Brown's satin shirt and Eric Clapton's guitar. People watching is great at the high stakes gaming area.

other highlights

Hotel guests wanting privacy at the enticing pool can reserve a chickee — a Seminole thatched enclosure — decked out with TVs, refrigerators and other cool toys. Get your body and mind in shape at the Rock Spa or shop at The Rainmaker retail store, which features Native American treasures including baskets and hand-made Seminole jewelry.

Seminole Hard Rock Hotel & Casino
5223 North Orient Road
Tampa, Florida 33610
(813) 627-7625
Toll free: (866) 502-PLAY (7529)

Admission: *Free.*

Hours: *Open 24 hours. Call ahead for hotel reservations.*

www.seminolehardrock.com

directions

From Tampa, take Interstate 4 east to exit 6 (Orient Road). Make a left onto Orient, the casino is on the right.

unique design, fine food and an accommodating staff.

Ybor City Museum State Park

one man's vision

Hillsborough County – West Central Florida

Ybor City State Museum

Firefighters of long ago relax in front of Ybor casitas after a hard day's work. At left, Seventh Avenue, old Ybor City.

the trip

Experience the rich and colorful history of a society built around cigars inside the remarkable Ybor City Museum State Park which consists of the Ybor City Museum, the Casita, and the Garden. Don Vicente Martinez Ybor was born in Valencia, Spain in 1818. He spent many years in Cuba and Key West before coming to Tampa where he opened Ybor's first cigar factory in 1886. He is considered Tampa's first industrial baron.

what to see

The museum chronicles the story of Ybor and the diverse group of people who came here to live and work. A pleasant walking tour takes you to a *casita*, or little house. These early homes of cigar workers are called "shotgun houses" because of their long, narrow frames. In the late 1800s, they rented for $2.50 per week and sold for anywhere between $400 and $900.

other highlights

The Museum Store, located next door to the museum, offers visitors a wide variety of items related to the history and cultural heritage of Ybor City. Among the many selections you'll find hand-rolled cigars, cigar art, memorabilia, books, gifts and gift baskets.

Ybor City State Museum
1818 E. Ninth Avenue
Tampa, FL 33605
(813) 247-6323

Admission: *$3 per person, free for children 6 and younger. Saturday walking tours, $6 per person.*

Hours: *Daily 9 a.m. to 5 p.m. Saturday morning walking tours begin at 10:30 a.m. Accommodations on a first-come-first-serve basis. Reservations recommended. Call (813) 241-6554.*

www.ybormuseum.org

directions

Take Interstate 4 to exit 1 (21st Street) south to Palm Avenue. Turn right on Palm Avenue, then left on 19th Street. Turn right onto Ninth Avenue. The Ybor City Museum is in the center of the block up on the right.

a look at a world gone by.

The Columbia Restaurant

more than 100 years and going strong

The Patio Room is one of the Columbia's many dining areas.

The Columbia Restaurant

Frank Atura

The Columbia's famous flamenco dancers entertain patrons.

Hillsborough County – West Central Florida

the trip

It opened in 1905 as a small corner café and was frequented by local cigar workers. Today, the original Columbia Restaurant is in its fifth and sixth generation of family ownership. Founded by Cuban immigrant Casimiro Hernandez, Sr., it is Florida's oldest and largest Spanish restaurant. Some of the world's best known celebrities, athletes, entertainers and politicians have dined at The Columbia.

what to see

The original restaurant in Ybor City seats more than 1,700 people in 15 spacious dining rooms. The Gonzmart family, led by Casey and Richard Gonzmart, serves thousands of traditional Spanish and Cuban meals daily. Paella à la Valenciana and Red Snapper Alicanté are just two of the excellent entreés that bring back locals again and again. Check out the Spanish Flamenco Dancers, considered the best in all of Florida. The décor, which includes hundreds of hand-painted tiles depicting the fanciful world of Don Quixote, is simply astounding.

other highlights

Enjoy live jazz, tapas, spirits and, of course, buy the finest cigars. You can also visit one of five additional Columbia Restaurants, all a *One Tank Trip®* from the Tampa Bay area, in Clearwater Beach, Celebration, Sarasota, St. Augustine and St. Petersburg.

The Columbia Restaurant
2117 E. Seventh Avenue
Tampa, FL 33605
(813) 248-4961

Admission: *Free. Prices of menu items vary. See Web site for menu.*

Hours: *Daily 11 a.m. to 10 p.m. Monday through Thursday; 11 a.m. to 11 p.m. Friday and Saturday; noon to 9 p.m. Sunday.*

www.columbiarestaurant.com

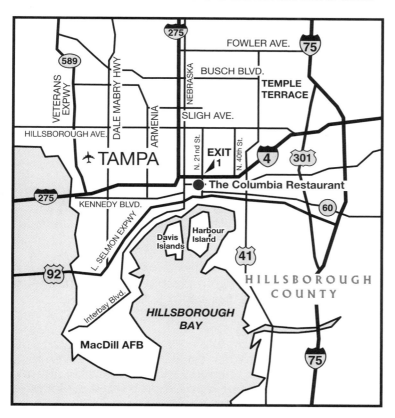

directions
Take Interstate 4 to exit 1 (21st Street) south to East Seventh Ave. The Columbia Restaurant is at the corner of East Seventh Ave. and 21st Street. Parking behind the restaurant or across the street.

enjoy the **foods of Spain** and **Cuba.**

Dinosaur World

giants of the past

Hillsborough County – West Central Florida

Dinosaur World

The tyrannosaurus rex (above) and the protoceratops (left), are two of more than 150 dinosaurs in Dinosaur World.

the trip

This former alligator farm has been transformed into the world's largest dinosaur attraction. The setting is a subtropical jungle, with dinosaurs around virtually every corner. This is a place for kids of all ages.

what to see

At this 12-acre outdoor museum you will walk among more than 150 life-size models of dinosaurs that roamed the earth during the Permian, Triassic, Cretaceous and Jurassic periods. You'll see stegosaurus, protoceratops, tyrannosaurus rex and many more! These remarkable fiberglass dinosaurs are made in Sweden.

other highlights

There are plenty of hands-on activities, such as fossil digs for the kids and a large playground. If you like, bring a picnic lunch and enjoy the cool shade of cypress, maple, gum and bay trees. And don't forget to pick up a unique souvenir from the gift shop.

Dinosaur World
5145 Harvey Tew Road
Plant City, FL 33565
(813) 717-9865

Admission: *$12.75 adults, $10.75 seniors older than 60, $9.75 children 3 to 12, free for children 2 and younger. Free parking.*

Hours: *Daily from 9 a.m. to 6 p.m. February through November; 9 a.m. to 5 p.m. December through January.*

www.dinoworld.net

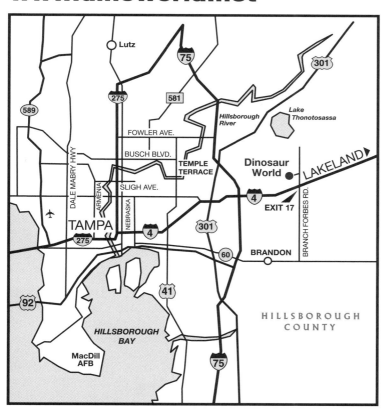

directions

Take Interstate 275 north to Interstate 4. Take exit 17 (Branch Forbes Road) turn left (north). Go under Interstate 4, then turn left almost immediately onto Harvey Tew Road. Go about 1500 feet and turn into the Dinosaur World parking lot.

Historic Plant City

more than just strawberries

Union Station Welcome Center

The former train depot has been converted into the Union Station Welcome Center. You can still get a Cherry Smash for a nickel at the Whistle Stop Café.

Michelle Newsome

Hillsborough County – West Central Florida

the trip

When you think of Plant City, chances are you think of the annual Florida Strawberry Festival. And what a delicious event it is! But there's much more. Named for railroad tycoon Henry Bradley Plant, historic Plant City has undergone a major restoration and downtown is the place to be.

what to see

Begin your tour at the Union Station Welcome Center on Palmer Street, which many years ago was the train depot. Today you can relive those famous railroad days at the Historic Train Depot and Museum. Pick up a downtown walking map to use as a guide. Take a stroll and explore the many shops and eateries in this neck of the woods. At the Whistle Stop Café, order a Cherry Smash for the old-fashioned price of a nickel! Oh, and don't forget about the Strawberry Festival, always held in late February or early March.

other highlights

Take a leisurely walk and glimpse into Plant City's fascinating past. Visit the 1914 high school and the many antique, collectibles, and specialty shops along the historic brick streets. Within these renovated buildings, you'll find shops such as Collins Street Junction, Frenchman's Market, Pieces of Olde, Marian Jones' Accents and Yesterdays Attic Antiques.

The Greater Plant City Chamber of Commerce
106 N. Evers Street
Plant City, FL 33563
(813) 754-3707
Toll free: (800) 760-2315

Admission: *Free.*

Hours: *Shop and restaurant hours vary. Call ahead for details.*

www.plantcity.org

directions

From Tampa, take Interstate 4 and head east to exit 19 at Thonotosassa Road (State Road 566 west). Make a slight right onto North Lemon Street. Turn left onto Baker Street (U.S. 92 east). Stay on 92 east to Historic Plant City.

there's **more** to this **charming** community **than** that **famous** berry.

Museum of Science & Industry (MOSI)

blinding you with science

Science comes alive at MOSI in unique and engaging ways, so keep your eyes peeled throughout your visit for learning games and various demonstrations.

MOSI

Hillsborough County – West Central Florida

the trip

The Museum of Science & Industry (MOSI) is the largest science center in the Southeastern United States and home to one of the only IMAX® Dome theaters in Florida. The Disasterville display combines education and 10,000 square feet of interactive exhibits with the remarkable science behind natural disasters. Kids in Charge! The Children's Science Center at MOSI is the largest children's science center in the nation.

what to see

You'll have to look real hard to find any "please do not touch" signs. Touching is not only allowed, it's encouraged! This is an interactive environment, with more than 450 hands-on activities for everyone. Take some time to explore our galaxy at The Saunders Planetarium. And be sure to see a Science Works Theater presentation.

other highlights

Pedal a bicycle balanced on a 1-inch steel cable, suspended 30 feet above the ground! This is the longest high wire bike in a United States museum and as death defying as this may sound, it's actually quite safe since the bike is counterweighted and a safety net is placed below the ride to set riders' minds at ease.

Museum of Science & Industry
4801 E. Fowler Avenue
Tampa, FL 33617
(813) 987-6300
Toll free: (800) 995-6674

Admission: *$23.95 adults, $21.95 seniors 60 and older, $19.95 children 2 to 13, free for children younger than 2.*

Hours: *9 a.m. to 5 p.m. Monday through Friday, 9 a.m. to 6 p.m. Saturday and Sunday.*

www.mosi.org

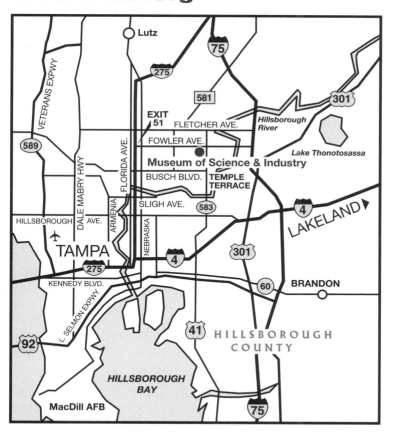

a real
hands on
approach to
science.

directions

Take Interstate 275 north to exit 51 east (Fowler Avenue /State Road 582A) then continue east for 3.5 miles. Turn right into MOSI.

Tampa Bay Downs Horse Racing Track

get your heart racing

Tom Cooley

A field of horses turning for the homestretch.

Hillsborough County – West Central Florida

the trip

Whether you come to place a bet or just enjoy the day, the 83-year-old Tampa Bay Downs Horse Racing Track is full of surprises.

what to see

The horses, of course! See and wager on both live and simulcast races from the grand stand, club house or veranda. Live racing takes place on a turf course over distances of one and-a-sixteenth and one-and-an-eighth miles.

other highlights

Whether you're betting or just here for fun, check out the races in style! Groups can reserve an exclusive Party Suite. Situated on the third floor, the private room features an exciting view of the finish line and great food. In the paddock you can get extremely close to the action! You can almost reach out and touch these beautiful horses as they are saddled and the jockeys mount up. The Silks Poker Room features cash poker tournament play. Golfers can enjoy The Downs Golf Practice Facility.

Tampa Bay Downs
11225 Race Track Road
Oldsmar, FL 34077
(813) 855-4401
Toll free: (800) 200-4434

Admission: *$2 general admission, $3 clubhouse. General parking is free, $2 preferred parking. Restaurant, bar and group rates vary.*

Hours: *Daily at 11 a.m. Closed Christmas and Easter.*

www.tampabaydowns.com

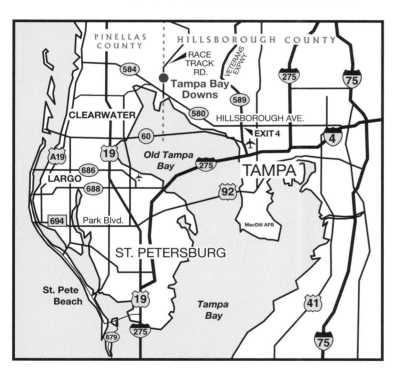

directions

From Tampa, take Interstate 275 south to the Tampa Airport exit. Follow signs to Veterans Expressway. Take Expressway north to exit 4 (Hillsborough Ave). Make a left on Hillsborough Avenue (west). Proceed approximately 10 miles to Race Track Road. Make a right on Race Track Road. Travel 1 mile to Tampa Bay Downs.

bet on
having **a**
great day!

Hillsborough County – West Central Florida

Tampa Theatre

have you ever visited a palace?

Tampa Theatre

The architectural detail and grandeur of the Tampa Theatre is unparalleled among grand movie palaces.

the trip

The magnificent Tampa Theatre is one of the nation's best-preserved examples of grand movie palace architecture. Built in 1926, it is listed on the National Register of Historic Places. In its early years, it presented extravagant vaudeville shows, concerts by its own orchestra and silent films.

what to see

Built as a silent film house by renowned architect John Eberson, the theater is a combination of Italian Renaissance, Byzantine, Greek Revival, English Tudor and more. It all works beautifully! The theater hosts some 700 events per year, including first-run and classic films, live shows, special events and tours.

other highlights

The Tampa Theatre experience is seeing and hearing The Mighty Wurlitzer Organ. It has more than 1,000 pipes; some are 16-feet tall, others are the size of pencils. The theater also boasts incredibly ornate plasterwork and a design style described as "Florida-Mediterranean."

The Tampa Theatre
711 N. Franklin Street
Tampa, FL 33602
(813) 274-8981

Admission: *Film tickets $9 adults, $7 seniors and military, $8 students, $5 backstage tours. Free for children younger than 12.*

Hours: *Check Web site, or call for film and event times.*

www.tampatheatre.org

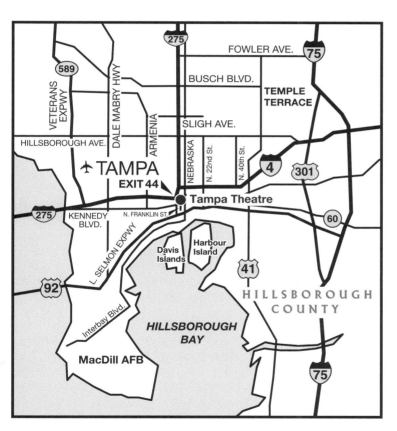

this theater **is** absolutely **exquisite!**

directions

Take Interstate 275 to exit 44 (Downtown/ West). Merge onto North Ashley Drive, then turn left onto East Zack Street. Park near the corner of Zack and Franklin streets (no cars are permitted on Franklin Street).

Renaissance Vinoy Resort & Golf Club

step into the Golden Age of Florida resorts

"Pretty in pink," the "Vinoy" is one of the West Coast's most elegant resorts. The dining rooms serve luscious Mediterranean cuisine.

Pinellas County – West Central Florida

the trip

Located on Tampa Bay's sparkling waterfront, the Mediterranean Revival-style Renaissance Vinoy Resort and Golf Club is a stunning pink and pretty sight. Listed on the National and Local Register of Historic Places and a member of the Historic Hotels of America, it is the grandest of the 1920's "boom era" hotels, and is still one of Florida's premier luxury resorts. For more than 80 years it has been the destination for dining, charity events, weddings, conventions and recreation.

what to see

An exploration of the historic lobby is a revelation. Redecorated and renovated it offers a History Gallery with a comprehensive display. The Vinoy is one of the only hotels in the country that has a full time historian on staff. Guided history tours with luncheon at Marchand's Bar & Grill are offered four days a week.

other highlights

The Vinoy offers guests amenities such as an 18-hole golf course, a 74-slip marina, two swimming pools, full-service health club, day spa, award-winning restaurants and lounges and a 12-court tennis complex. The Vinoy is also within walking distance to St. Petersburg's Museum of Fine Arts and the Salvador Dali Museum.

The Renaissance Vinoy Resort & Golf Club
501 5th Avenue Northeast
St. Petersburg, Florida 33701
(727) 894-1000
Toll free: (888) 303-4430

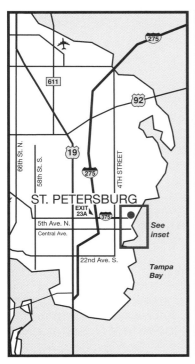

Admission: *History tour and luncheon is $22.95. Hotel accommodation prices vary.*

Hours: *History and luncheon tours depart at 10:30 a.m. from the Concierge Desk on Wednesday through Saturday.*

www.renaissancevinoyresort.com

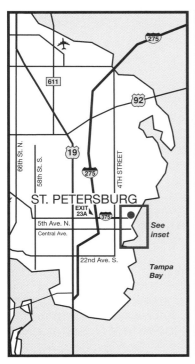

directions

From Tampa, take Interstate 275 south to exit 23-A (Interstate 375) in St. Petersburg. Stay left, follow 4th Avenue North to Beach Drive, turn left. The resort is one block on the right.

Pinellas County – West Central Florida

BayWalk

take a walk on the wonderful side

Restaurants, movies, shopping and entertainment – BayWalk is helping to change the face of downtown St. Pete.

BayWalk

the trip

BayWalk is a growing part of blossoming downtown St. Pete, and it will turn your head! Muvico 20, a magnificent 20-screen theater, is the main focus for many visitors. But there's quite a bit more, including dining, shopping, entertainment in the courtyard and live music on the weekends. The $40-million, 125,000-square-foot outdoor complex takes up an entire city block. And, as the name suggests, it's just a short walk to the bay, where you can visit the renowned Museum of Fine Arts (255 Beach Drive N.E.) and the beautiful Sculpture Gardens.

what to see

For starters, kick back at Wet Willie's Daiquiri Bar (non-alcoholic beverages are available here, too). You will get a birds-eye view of the crowd below from Willie's perch on the second floor. Want munchies? Rock out to a '50s burger and fries at Johnny Rockets. Or stop for a bite at TooJay's Gourmet Deli, a New York-style delicatessen with a great selection of to-die-for pastries.

other highlights

Visit fine retailers such as Ann Taylor, Chico's, and White House/Black Market, which carry trendy lines of clothing. It's Ben & Jerry's for fantastic ice cream and candies. While in the neighborhood, take a stroll over to The Pier for more shops and eateries, like the world-famous Columbia Restaurant. Browse the fancy boutique shops at nearby Beach Drive.

BayWalk
Corner of First Street N. & Second Avenue N.
St. Petersburg, FL 33701
(727) 895-9277

Admission: *Free.*

Hours: *Restaurant and shop hours vary. For movie times and prices, call Muvico at (727) 502-0965 or visit the Web site at www.muvico.com.*

www.yourbaywalk.com

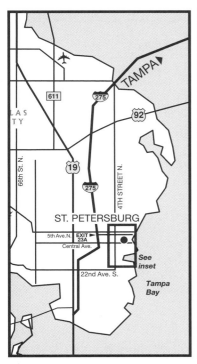

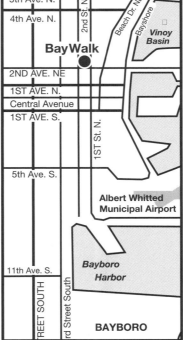

directions

From Tampa, take Interstate 275 south to exit 23-A (Interstate 375 east). Merge onto Fourth Avenue North, then turn right onto Second Street North. BayWalk is to your left on the corner of First Street North and Second Avenue North. The parking garage is located on Second Street North; there is minimal parking on the street.

this **area of**
St. Pete
has something
for **everyone.**

Pinellas County – West Central Florida

The Chattaway Restaurant

early St. Pete ambiance

H. Little

D. Graphics

The Chattaway Restaurant is famous for its mouth-watering "Chattaburgers" all-the-way. Dine alfresco amid the 44 Cracker-style tubs planted with a colorful variety of Florida flowers.

the trip

This taste-tempting landmark has been around for most of the 20th century and is making a good start into the 21st. The little wooden building once housed a grocery store, gas station and trolley stop. When the building changed hands in 1950, it was turned into a full-fledged restaurant and the Chattaway was born.

what to see

The Chattaway's casual charm is further embellished by an enclosed verandah and a charming tea room. As for the food, try the famed "Chattaburger" (with all the fixings) and equally-famed onion rings. Many locals say it's the best burger in town.

other highlights

Be sure to ask about the daily specials. While waiting for your chow, take time to admire the huge collection of British collectibles throughout the restaurant.

The Chattaway Restaurant
358 22nd Avenue S.
St. Petersburg, FL 33705
(727) 823-1594

Admission: *Free. Prices of menu items vary.*

Hours: *Daily 11 a.m. to 9:30 p.m.*

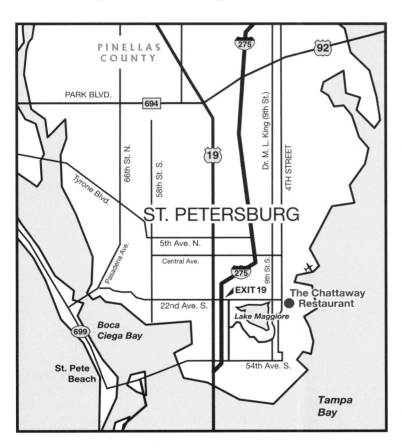

directions

From Tampa, take Interstate 275 south (towards Bradenton) to the 22nd Avenue South exit (exit 19). Head east all the way to 4th Street South. The Chattaway Restaurant is located on the southeast corner of 22nd Avenue South and Fourth Street South, across the street from Bartlett Park.

casual charm meets good eats.

Pinellas County – West Central Florida

Florida Holocaust Museum

a time to remember

J. LaFray

The Florida Holocaust Museum houses many compelling exhibits depicting the history, heritage and hope of the people subjected to Nazi persecution and hate.

the trip

It is a journey of major historical significance at the Florida Holocaust Museum. As one of the largest Holocaust museums in the southeast, it offers a powerful and sobering exploration of our past.

what to see

Here you will experience the dreams, achievements and convictions of the 11-million innocent victims of Nazi tyranny. The centerpiece has a number — 1130695-5. It is one of the few remaining railroad boxcars used by the Nazis to transport victims to concentration camps. In another part of the museum are shoes that belonged to a two-year-old child who died with her mother in Auschwitz in 1943.

other highlights

Be sure to visit the wall of tiles, created mostly by children who have visited the museum. Part of the museum's education outreach includes The Speakers' Bureau, where Holocaust survivors, serving as eyewitnesses to history, share their stories. The museum also offers literature-based "Teaching Trunks," with lessons on the Holocaust for grades K through 12.

The Florida Holocaust Museum
55 Fifth Street S.
St. Petersburg, FL 33701
(727) 820-0100

Admission: *$12 adults, $10 seniors and college students, $6 for children younger than 18.*

Hours: *Daily 10 a.m. to 5 p.m. Closed Rosh Hashana, Yom Kippur, Thanksgiving, Christmas Day and New Year's Day.*

www.flholocaustmuseum.org

directions

From Tampa, take Interstate 275 south to exit 23-A (Interstate 375) and follow the signs to Fourth Avenue North. Turn right onto Fifth Street North for about three blocks. Turn into the marked alleyway directing you to the to parking lot.

images... that must never be forgotten.

Florida Orange Groves & Winery

wines with a twist

Florida Orange Groves & Winery, Inc.

For many years the Shook family (l. to r.) Ray, Gladys and Vince, have been producing delicious citrus wines.

Pinellas County – West Central Florida

the trip

There's just one type of grape in a bunch at Florida's only citrus winery! It's made with a native grape – muscadine – and it's organically grown. You'll want to savor a taste along with the other fine citrus wines produced here. The tours and tastings are always a treat and the gift shop is just packed with goodies.

what to see

What's this? Cranberry, watermelon, tangerine and Key lime wine? That's right, and there's more, including the award-winning cherry, carrot and blackberry wines. Part of your tour includes a look at the Shook family's state-of-the-art winemaking operation. The Florida Citrus Commission awarded citrus winemakers the right to display the "Florida Sunshine Tree" logo on their labels. It's the first time that the Citrus Commission has allowed its mark on a beverage other than orange or grapefruit juice.

other highlights

This winery is not only for oenophiles (i.e. wine lovers). There are plenty of other libations here, many without a hint of alcohol. Fresh orange and grapefruit juice are processed daily. While in the area, visit Ted Peters Smoked Fish restaurant just up the street (1350 Pasadena Ave.) for some of the best smoked fish and burgers around.

Florida Orange Groves & Winery
1500 Pasadena Avenue S.
St. Petersburg, FL 33707
(727) 347-4025
Toll free: (800) 338-7923

Admission: *Free. Prices of wines vary.*

Hours: *Monday through Saturday 9 a.m. to 5:30 p.m., Sunday 12 p.m. to 5 p.m. Tastings available daily. Call for details and tour times.*

www.floridawine.com

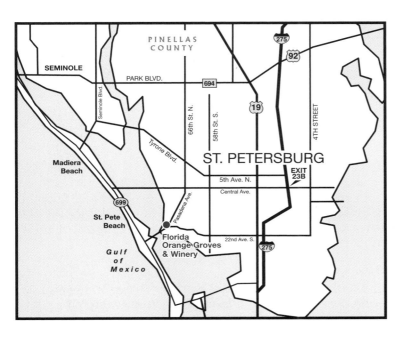

directions
From Tampa, take Interstate 275 south to Fifth Avenue North (exit 23-B) in St. Petersburg. Turn right (heading west) onto Fifth Avenue North and go to 66th Street North. Turn left (south) on 66th Street North which turns into Pasadena Avenue. Continue south, until you see the winery on the left, just before the causeway to St. Pete Beach.

Pinellas County's **only** winery!

Pinellas County – West Central Florida

John's Pass Village & Boardwalk

it takes a village!

This quaint turn-of-the-century fishing village has become a popular tourist attraction with more than a hundred merchants, a variety of restaurants and a host of outdoor sports to entertain.

J. Groth

the trip

At first glance you might think you've arrived at an old New England fishing village. It certainly has all the rustic charm. But quaint John's Pass Village & Boardwalk is a lot more than that. It's a bonanza of retail, recreational and restaurant venues.

what to see

Along the boardwalk there are many days' worth of things to see and do. Jack's Marina is one of several places offering boat and watercraft rentals. You can go parasailing, deep-sea fishing, shell hunting, sailing and even dolphin watching. And, if you feel lucky, the casino boats are here too, offering daily excursions. Hungry? The seafood restaurants are outstanding. The Friendly Fisherman has also been luring locals for years. For real New York-style pizza, stop at DeLosa's Pizzeria right at the entrance to the boardwalk.

other highlights

Gift shops abound, including FLA Mingos, Raptors and Relics, Sugar Daddy's, Wild Time and the Unique Boutique. One of the new arrivals on the boardwalk is Thomas Kinkade Gallery, featuring the works of the beloved "Painter of Light."

John's Pass Village & Boardwalk
12901 Gulf Boulevard E.
Madeira Beach, FL 33708

Gulf Beaches
Chamber of Commerce
Toll free: (800) 944-1847

Admission: *Free.*

Hours: *Shop and restaurant hours vary.*

www.johnspass.com

you won't **get** bored on the **boardwalk.**

directions

From Tampa, take Interstate 275 south to exit 28 (Pinellas Park/Gandy Blvd.). Follow Gandy Blvd., which becomes Park Blvd. (County Road 694 west), to the end. Turn left onto Gulf Blvd. Follow Gulf Blvd. for about 5 miles to John's Pass Village.

Marine Life Adventures

an interactive marine experience

Pinellas County – West Central Florida

Marianne Klingel

Sea Life Safari Cruises leave from the Clearwater Marine Aquarium's marina. Left, a young adventurer examines the catch of the otter trawl before releasing it to the Bay.

the trip

Here's your opportunity to learn something new while having fun. Through "fun education," see first-hand the amazing and important work being accomplished at this non-profit, working animal hospital. The goal is to rescue, rehabilitate and release marine life back into the wild. Winter, the dolphin that has an artificial tail, is the most amazing rescue story of them all. Come visit this resilient and internationally-known dolphin who has become friend to thousands.

what to see

The Aquarium offers exhibits and presentations with dolphins, sea turtles, river otters and more. You can also touch a stingray, get your picture taken with a dolphin and even be a dolphin trainer for a day. The Aquarium also offers an IMAX®-style theater and an underwater dolphin viewing tunnel.

other highlights

The Clearwater Marine Aquarium offers Sea Life Safari Cruises, kayak trips and much more. Daily cruises are narrated by a biologist and offer guests an opportunity to explore local waterways, while learning about how everyone plays a role in protecting our marine life environment.

Clearwater Marine Aquarium
249 Windward Passage
Clearwater, FL 33767
(727) 441-1790
Toll free: (888) 239-9414

Admission: *$11 adults, $7.50 children 3 to 12, $9 seniors. For Sea Life Safari: $21.35 adults, $19.95 seniors, $13.75 children 3 to 12.*

Hours: *The aquarium is open Monday through Thursday 9 a.m. to 5 p.m., Friday and Saturday 9 a.m. to 9 p.m., Sunday 10 a.m. to 5 p.m.*

www.seewinter.com

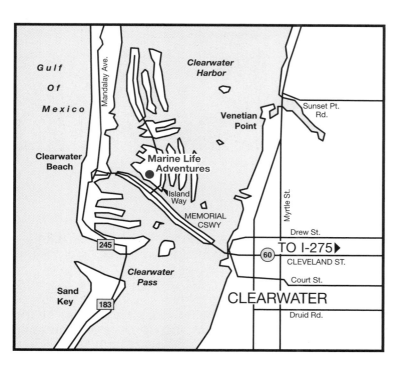

your
window
to the
sea.

directions

From Tampa, take Interstate 275 south to State Road 60 west. Cross over the Courtney Campbell Causeway which becomes Gulf-to-Bay Boulevard and then Cleveland Street. Once over the causeway, turn right (north) onto Island Way. Turn left at Windward Passage.

Tarpon Springs Aquarium

wet, wild and wondrous

Pinellas County – West Central Florida

Children love the touch tank where they can actually make contact with its inhabitants and learn the proper way to feed them. At right, Cloey — the resident 14-foot python — delights young visitors.

Tarpon Springs Aquarium

the trip

You'll see more than 30 species of coastal sea creatures including a 200-pound Goliath Grouper and nurse sharks in this fascinating aquarium that opened its doors in 1990.

what to see

Learn about fearsome alligators and alligator snapping turtles at the alligator feeding shows. And don't miss getting up close and personal with Cloey — the 14-foot python. There's a touch tank for children where aquarium workers teach children the right and wrong way to feed and pet rays.

other highlights

If the shark feeding makes you hungry, be sure to explore Tarpon Spring's dining delights for humans. Settled by Greek immigrants, there are still restaurants that offer Greek food just down the street from the aquarium.

Tarpon Springs Aquarium
850 Dodecanese Blvd.
Tarpon Springs, FL 34689
(727) 938-5378

Admission: *$5.75 adults, $5 seniors, $3.75 children (3 to 11), free for children 3 and younger.*

Hours: *Monday through Saturday 10 a.m. to 5 p.m., Sunday noon to 5 p.m.*

www.tarponspringsaquarium.com

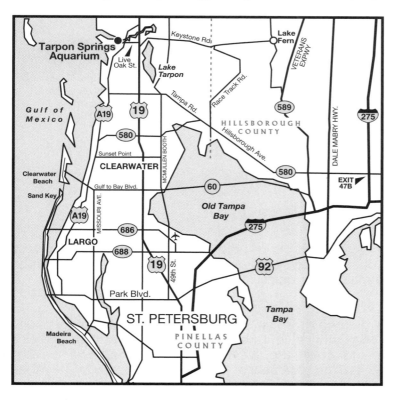

directions

From Tampa, take Interstate 275 north to the Hillsborough Avenue/U.S. 92 west exit, 47-B. Merge onto East Hillsborough Avenue, which becomes Tampa Road. Turn right onto U.S. 19 north. Make a slight left onto East Live Oak Street. Stay straight to go onto Dodecanese Boulevard.

have you hugged a **shark** today?

Pinellas County – West Central Florida

The Town of Safety Harbor

the secret by the bay

The elegant facade of the Safety Harbor Resort & Spa sets the tone for the pampering to follow.

Sue Suby, Tropical Breeze Publications, Inc.

the trip

It may be the Town of Safety Harbor, but a glance at Main Street and you get the feeling of a quaint little village. The world-famous Safety Harbor Resort & Spa, a magnet for many celebrities, stands at the east end.

what to see

There are more than 40 shops and restaurants and several lovely parks. Spend some time enjoying the beauty of the waterfront at the city marina. Across and down the street is the Safety Harbor Museum, where they say you can experience "10,000 years of history." Farther down Main Street, stop at Syd Entel Galleries, a Safety Harbor mainstay for more than 20 years. The visual celebration continues at Susan Benjamin Glass. Original painting, sculptures and signed prints are a veritable feast for the eyes.

other highlights

On the third Friday of the month, Main Street becomes a pedestrian mall. Vendors of art, jewelry and crafts display their wares and there is live music at the gazebo.

Safety Harbor Chamber of Commerce
200 Main Street
Safety Harbor, FL 34695
(727) 726-2890

Admission: *Free.*

Hours: *Shop and restaurant hours vary.*

www.safetyharborchamber.com

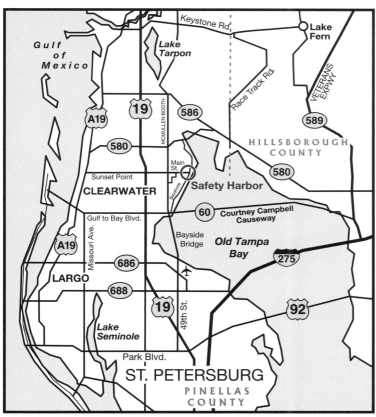

directions

From Tampa, take State Road 60 west to Clearwater over the Courtney Campbell Causeway which becomes Gulf to Bay Boulevard. Bear to the right (north) on McMullen-Booth Road to Main Street. Turn right (east) onto Main Street and follow to the center of the town of Safety Harbor.

all **signs** point **to** a **fun** day in Safety Harbor.

Shell Key Shuttle

like Gilligan's Island, but you get to go home

Hop aboard for a trip to
the sparkling white sands
of Shell Key.

Pinellas County – West Central Florida

the trip

From St. Pete Beach's Merry Pier, take a 10-minute catamaran shuttle to Shell Key. It's a beautiful, unspoiled barrier island just south of Pass-a-Grille, at the southern end of St. Pete Beach.

what to see

You might have guessed that Shell Key got its name because it's a great place to find some spectacular shells. But there's plenty else to do, like watching the birds (the Key is a bird preservation area). Sunbathing and snorkeling are also high on the list. Umbrellas, snorkels and masks are provided, but bring your own cooler and a bag for collecting shells. And check out the shell chart on your way back to identify your finds!

other highlights

Back on dry land, pop across the street and enjoy historic Pass-a-Grille's Eighth Avenue. You can browse several shops and drop in for breakfast or lunch at the Seahorse Restaurant. For breakfast, head slightly west to the Gulf to enjoy a fresh fruit plate or full English breakfast at the outdoor Seaside Grill (900 Gulf Way), located directly on the Gulf of Mexico.

Merry Pier at Pass-a-Grille
801 Pass-a-Grille Way
St. Pete Beach, FL 33706
(727) 360-1348

Admission: *Round-trip shuttle fares, $22 adults, $11 children 12 and younger.*

Hours: *The Shell Key Shuttle departs from Merry Pier daily at 10 a.m., noon, and 2 p.m. and returns at 12:15 p.m., 2:15 p.m. and 4:15 p.m.*

www.shellkeyshuttle.com

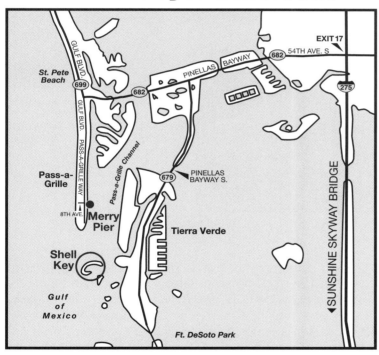

directions

From Tampa, take Interstate 275 south to exit 17 (Pinellas Bayway/St. Pete Beach/State Road 682). Go about three miles (through the toll booth) to Gulf Boulevard. Turn left and follow Gulf Boulevard, which becomes Pass-a-Grille Way. Follow to the Merry Pier which is on Pass-a-Grille Channel at 8th Avenue on the left side of the road. Park on the street, but don't feed the meter. Obtain a city-parking pass for $2.

a **shell** hunter's **dream.**

Suncoast Seabird Sanctuary

this hospital is for the birds

Suncoast Seabird Sanctuary

An injured brown pelican gets some tender loving care. Left, these baby brown pelicans were hatched in the safety of the sanctuary.

the trip

The Suncoast Seabird Sanctuary is the largest wild bird hospital in the nation. Founded in 1971 by zoologist Ralph Heath, Jr., the sanctuary rescues, treats and releases as many as 10,000 sick and injured wild birds.

what to see

You can see more than 600 birds, including egrets, cormorants, brown pelicans and various birds of prey. On an average day, Ralph and the folks at the sanctuary treat about two dozen birds injured by gunshots, fishing hooks and lines. While the sanctuary's goal is to release the birds after they have recuperated from their injuries, some who have lost an eye or a limb, remain here in permanent residence.

other highlights

Located on the Gulf Coast near St. Petersburg, the sanctuary is well suited for bird-watching. Many guests stroll the grounds and enjoy the opportunities for photography.

Pinellas County – West Central Florida

Suncoast Seabird Sanctuary
18328 Gulf Boulevard
Indian Shores, FL 33785
(727) 391-6211

Admission: *Free. Contributions are appreciated.*

Hours: *Daily 9 a.m. to sunset.*

www.seabirdsanctuary.com

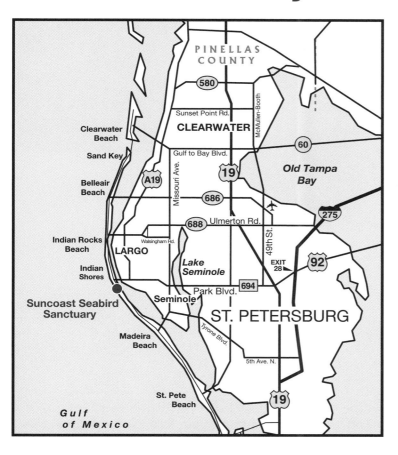

this is a
wonderful
daytime
destination,
and **you'll**
never know
what surprises
await.

directions

From Tampa, take Interstate 275 south to exit 28 (County Road 694). Merge onto Gandy Boulevard north, which becomes Park Boulevard. Go about 10 miles and turn left onto Gulf Boulevard. The Suncoast Seabird Sanctuary is at Mile Marker 13, less than a mile on the right.

TRIP 39

Sunken Gardens

a tropical downtown paradise

Sunken Gardens

The tropical paradise is home to these resident parrots who appear to enjoy the spectacular beauty of Sunken Gardens as much as everyone else.

the trip

Not so long ago, this landmark attraction drew 300,000 visitors a year. But because of declining attendance, the owners opted to sell the place. That could have meant the end of Sunken Gardens, but St. Petersburg voters gave thumbs up for the city to buy and operate the Gardens. And now, the transformation from an "attraction" to an educational and cultural center is complete.

what to see

Check out the Gardens' latest additions. There are more than 6,000 new plants, and an aviary. There's also a rain forest information center where you'll see some remarkable critters, such as snakes and green lizards. Yet, much of the old Sunken Gardens remains.

other highlights

There are many interesting activities such as horticultural programs, guided tours and festivals including an orchid festival. Check out Great Explorations for the kids — great hands-on fun!

Sunken Gardens
1825 Fourth Street N.
St. Petersburg, FL 33704
(727) 551-3100

Admission: *$8 adults, $6 seniors, $4 children 2 to 11.*

Hours: *Monday through Saturday 10 a.m. to 4:30 p.m., Sunday noon to 4:30 p.m. Closed Thanksgiving and Christmas.*

www.sunkengardens.org

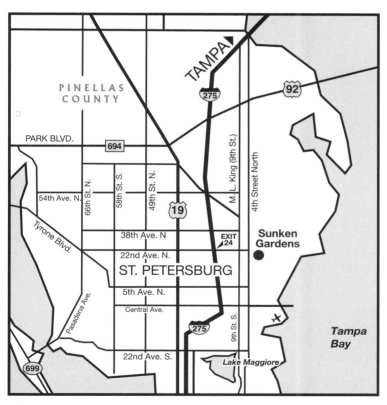

directions

From Tampa, take Interstate 275 south to St. Petersburg. Take exit 24 (22nd Avenue North). Turn left and head east on 22nd Avenue North and follow it to Fourth Street North. Turn right on Fourth Street North. Sunken Gardens is less than a half-mile on the left.

you'll be **awed** by the beauty and **tranquility** of these **lovely** gardens.

Pinellas County – West Central Florida

Derby Lane

on track with fastest greyhounds

Derby Lane

Here Comes Rusty! is the cry that sets the greyhounds to their paces at exciting live action racing.

the trip

This venerable track has been a premier dog-racing venue since 1925 and is the longest, continuously operating dog track in the world. Such luminaries as Babe Ruth, Lou Gehrig and Dizzy Dean have visited the track, but more recently Derby was the backdrop for the theatrical movie "Ocean's Eleven" with stars George Clooney and Brad Pitt.

what to see

A picturesque array of Florida flora that attracts exotic birds and other feathered wildlife, surrounds the track. Simulcast jai alai, greyhound, thoroughbred and harness races supplement the live-action racing card.

other highlights

In addition to the exciting dog races, Derby Lane also boasts a large poker room where Texas Hold 'Em, Seven Card Stud, Omaha and other games are played. Check out the Web site for tournament times. In addition, the track also hosts concerts and other special events. Hungry? The track's dining venues are well known and include Derby Club Restaurant which affords a superb view of the dog races. Visit the gift shop stocked with greyhound racing mementos and souvenirs.

Derby Lane
10490 Gandy Boulevard
St. Petersburg, FL 33702
(727) 812-3339

Admission: *Free parking, free valet optional.*

Hours: *Matinee post time 12:30 p.m. Wednesday, Saturday. Evening post time 7:30 p.m. Monday through Saturday. Note that track days and times are subject to change, call or visit the Web site to verify the current racing and poker schedules.*

www.derbylane.com

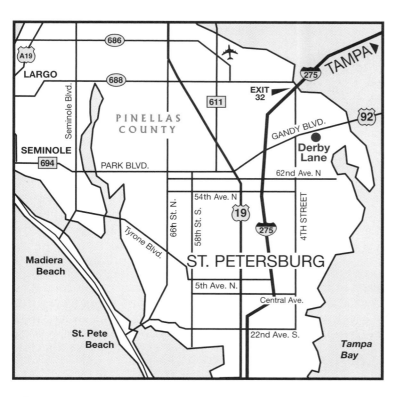

directions
From Tampa, take Interstate 275 south across the Howard Frankland Bridge to exit 32 (4th Street) and follow south to Gandy Blvd. Turn left and head east on Gandy Blvd. for about 1/4 mile. Derby Lane is on the right.

Manatee County – West Central Florida

Florida Railroad Museum

all aboard!

Florida Gulf Coast Railroad Museum

Built in 1951 and donated to the museum by the Department of Defense, both the #1822 and #1835, which sports the Florida Gulf Coast Museum logo, are 1500 horsepower locomotives.

the trip

Train lovers—get ready! You will ride through rustic Manatee County prairie land on this moving exhibit. Operated entirely by volunteers, the museum was founded in 1981 to acquire, protect and operate historic examples of the line. Opened in 1903, it was known as the Florida & West Indies Railroad & Steamship Company.

what to see

These diesel-powered trains include open-window coaches, air-conditioned coach and lounge cars and cabooses. From Parrish, your trip takes you to Willow, once the location of a large logging mill. Farther along, the train stops at Nichols Station, surrounded by cypress trees in a swamp that seems out of place in this prairie setting. Keep an eye out for alligators, deer, turtles and many birds along the way. And depending on the day, you might even encounter masked bandits!

other highlights

Want more fun? The museum will rent out a locomotive on an hourly basis, complete with an instructor to demonstrate the controls. After a brief instruction period, you'll be running the locomotive yourself! When finished, you receive an honorary locomotive engineer certificate suitable for framing.

Florida Railroad Museum
U.S. 301 & 83rd Street E.
Parrish, FL 34219
Toll free: (877) 869-0800

Admission: *$12 adults, $8 children 3 to 11. Call for group rates. Locomotive rental and birthday caboose charter available.*

Hours: *Trains depart 11 p.m. and 2 p.m. Saturday and Sunday. Closed Easter weekend and the weekend between Christmas and New Year's Day.*

www.frrm.org

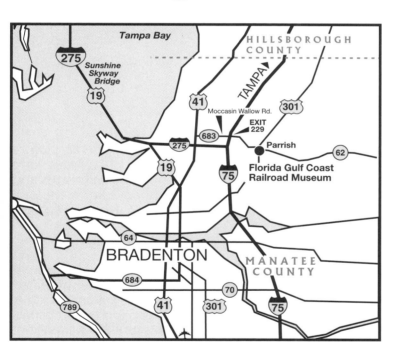

directions

From Tampa, take Interstate 75 south to exit 229 (Moccasin Wallow Road/State Road 683). Head east toward U.S. 301 for about 5 miles. Turn right (south) on U.S. 301 and go about one-quarter of a mile. Turn left at 83rd Street East. Go one short block to the parking lot.

Anna Maria Island

touch your toes on sugar-white sands

Have a quick bite while taking in the magnificent views of Anna Maria Island. Right, enjoy a catamaran ride to many of the fine beaches on Anna Maria Island.

Bradenton Area CVB

the trip

This "Island in the Sun" has a long history as a vacation destination as well as a pleasant place to day trip. The seven-and-a-half-mile long island, discovered by the Timucan and Caloosan American Indians and Spanish explorers, including the famed Hernando de Soto, consists of three scenic cities: Anna Maria, Holmes Beach and Bradenton Beach.

what to see

Visit the Anna Maria Island Historical Society to view photos of the island as it once was. It has been the picturesque setting for several Hollywood movies. A walk around the island is the best way to see the shell-lined sugar-white shores, tropical birds and other amazing island wildlife. Savor the elegant restaurants and beachside pubs. Sports enthusiasts will rejoice at the inshore and offshore sport fishing, parasailing, kayaking, bicycling and canoeing. The Anna Maria pier is the perfect place for an early morning breakfast. Fresh seafood is always available.

other highlights

Spend an evening with the Island Players live theatre after dinner at the acclaimed Beach Bistro, famous for fresh seafood dining overlooking the Gulf. Nearby attractions include the South Florida Museum and Aquarium, the Ringling Museum of Art, Selby Gardens, Mote Marine Aquarium and the Asolo Center for the Performing Arts.

Anna Maria Island Chamber of Commerce
5313 Gulf Drive N.
Holmes Beach, FL 34217
(941) 778-1541

Admission: *Beaches are free.*

www.annamariaislandchamber.org

a vacation destination like no other.

directions
From Tampa, take Interstate 75 south to exit 220, heading west on State Road 64 (Manatee Avenue) into Bradenton and the Anna Maria Island Beaches.

Roaring 20's Pizza & Pipes

a tasty, easy-on-the-ears destination

Manatee County – West Central Florida

Roaring 20s Pizza and Pipes

The Mighty Wurlitzer is a sight and sound to behold.

the trip

At Ellenton's Roaring 20's the main focus is twofold—mighty good pizza and The Mighty Wurlitzer organ. This is a remarkable one-of-a-kind place.

what to see

The names of the pizzas set the tone for this place—The Charlie Chaplin, The Buster Keaton, The Bees Knees and The Mighty Wurlitzer—wait until you see what they put on this pie! Not in the mood for pizza? Try a sandwich or a pasta selection, and finish your feast with a big scoop of ice cream.

other highlights

Now on to the other star of the show — the music! The Mighty Wurlitzer began its life at Oakland's Paramount Theatre in 1931, and found its way here in 1999. It was no easy task. It took 2,600 hours to rebuild, then another 1,700 to install the 16-ton organ. A 20 horsepower blower supplies air for its 3,000 pipes. Amazingly, the Wurlitzer has 26 miles of wiring and 350 controls! Also, good luck trying to stump the organists with what you think is an unusual song request. These guys know just about everything! Talk about a great family destination!

Roaring 20's Pizza & Pipes
6750 N. U.S. 301
Ellenton, FL 34222
(941) 723-1733

Admission: *Free. Prices of menu items vary.*

Hours: *Tuesday through Saturday 4:30 p.m. to 8:30 p.m., Friday 4:30 p.m. to 9 p.m., Saturday noon to 2:30 p.m. and 4:30 p.m. to 10 p.m. Closed for all major holidays.*

www.roaring20spizza.com

directions

From Tampa, head south on Interstate 75 to exit 224 (U.S. 301/Ellenton/Palmetto). Merge left onto U.S. 301 north, then follow the road for about three-quarters of a mile. Roaring 20's Pizza and Pipes is on the north side of U.S. 301.

your Roaring 20's experience should be a roaring success.

Rosa Fiorelli Winery

full-bodied adventure

Rosa Fiorelli Winery accommodates wine tastings, weddings and other festive functions.

The Fiorellis proudly display their award-winning wines.

Rosa Fiorelli Winery

the trip
It started out as five rows of grapes in the backyard. Today, it has swelled to more than ten acres! It all began when Rosa and Antonio Fiorelli relocated here from Sicily and opened Manatee County's first winery on a quiet little road in Bradenton, just south of Lake Manatee.

what to see
Your visit will include a tour of the vineyard. You will learn about the different varieties of grapes, growth seasons, pruning and harvesting times. Then see how grapes are crushed, pressed, fermented and bottled. All followed with a delightful wine tasting.

other highlights
Bring home some *vino!* Depending on the season, nine different varieties are available, from the full-bodied Manatee Red to the sweet Florida Muscadine, nicknamed the "*amoré* wine," or "love wine." The *Blanc du Bois Classico* is an international award winner.

Rosa Fiorelli Winery
4250 County Road 675
Bradenton, FL 34211
(941) 322-0976

Admission: *Lunch tours, which include a souvenir wine glass, are $16.70 per person including gratuity. Regular tours of the winery and vineyards are $5 per person. Wine tastings and wine and cheese tours are free.*

Hours: *Monday through Wednesday, Saturday 10 a.m. to 6 p.m., Sunday noon to 5 p.m. Closed Tuesday.*

www.fiorelliwinery.com

directions
From Tampa, take Interstate 75 south to exit 220 (State Road 64). Go east about 10 miles to County Road 675. Turn right into the winery.

a tasty mom-and-pop operation.

Royal Lipizzan Stallions of Austria

extraordinary grace

Manatee County – West Central Florida

For four months each year, hundreds of equine lovers flock to see the Lipizzan stallions drill.

B. Murphy

the trip

You can see these magnificent horses in training for only the first four months of the year. And while it may look like a real performance, part of the training of the young stallions is to get comfortable in front of an audience. It all takes place under the close direction of Gabriella Herrmann, daughter of the late Colonel Ottomar Herrmann, whose family has trained the Lipizzans for more than 300 years.

what to see

This is a rare opportunity to see the magnificent Royal Lipizzans up close. The stallions were saved from almost certain extinction at the end of World War II. Colonel Herrmann and his father smuggled their horses out of Europe under the protection of General George S. Patton. Decades later, these "original" Lipizzans are here for all to behold!

other highlights

It takes nine years for these horses to learn "the capriole," the move for which they are best known. Leaping from all four feet, they strike out with the hind legs. Once a battle maneuver of their ancestors, it is now part of this remarkable equine ballet.

Herrmanns'
Royal Lipizzan Stallions
32755 Singletary Road
Myakka City, FL 34251
(941) 322-1501

Admission: *Free. Reservations suggested for groups of 15 or more.*

Hours: *Winter training sessions take place at 3 p.m. on Thursdays and Fridays and 10 a.m. Saturdays beginning the first week of January and continuing through the end of April.*

www.hlipizzans.com

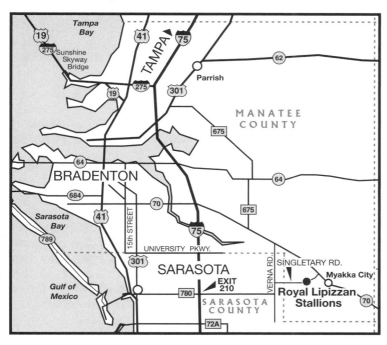

the **training** takes years, **beginning** when the stallions **turn** three.

directions

From Tampa, take Interstate 75 south to exit 210 (State Road 780 (Fruitville Road), which becomes Country Road 780 (still Fruitville Road). Follow to the end. Turn left (north) onto Verna Road. Turn right (east) onto Singletary Road. At the stop sign, turn right again to stay on Singletary Road. Hermanns' is on the left.

The John and Mable Ringling Museum of Art

museum complex extraordinaire

In 1925, New York architect John Phillips design a building befitting the Ringling's impressive art collection.

On display, left is "Hager and the Angel" (1637) in the Ringling Museum of Art.

The Ringling Museum

the trip

Talk about a feast for the eyes! There are more than five centuries of European art here including a world-famous collection of 17th century Baroque paintings. The nearby Circus Museum honors John Ringling and celebrates the success of the Ringling Bros. and Barnum & Bailey Circus.

what to see

A testament to John and Mable Ringling's love of art, the Museum of Art is considered one of the most attractive in the nation. John Ringling, an influential business tycoon and cultural baron of his day, bequeathed his valuable and extensive art collection, palazzo, gardens and grounds to the people of Florida. The 19th century art is splendid, and the museum actively collects 20th century and contemporary art. In the courtyard — a wonder to behold — bronze replicas of Baroque, Greek and Roman sculptures represent the nation's most complete collection of works by the Chiurazzi foundry in Naples, Italy.

other highlights

You will find the story of "The Greatest Show on Earth" in the Circus Museum. This is the first museum of its kind, with a collection that documents the history of the circus. Here you will see an antique parade wagon used to delight children in the 1920s and 1930s. Also on display are posters, costumes, handbills and miniature circuses. While there, be sure to visit the Ca' d'Zan, John Ringling's magnificent winter residence featured in the Volume I **One Tank Trips®** book.

John and Mable Ringling Museum of Art
5401 Bay Shore Road
Sarasota, FL 34243
(941) 359-5700
(941) 351-1660

Admission: *$19 adults, $16 seniors and active military personnel, $6 Florida students and teachers with valid IDs, free for children 6 and younger. Art Museum free on Mondays.*

Hours: *Daily 10 a.m. to 5:30 p.m. Closed Thanksgiving, Christmas and New Year's Day.*

www.ringling.org

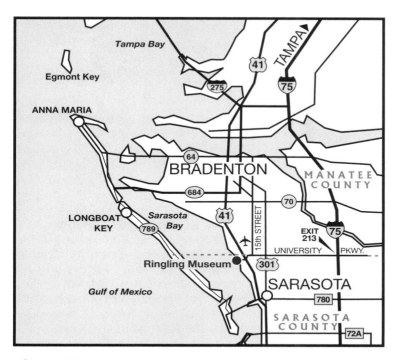

directions

From Tampa, take Interstate 75 south to exit 213. Merge onto University Parkway and follow to the end. The Ringling Museum is at the end of University Parkway which becomes Ringling Plaza.

a three-ring **experience.**

Crane Point Museum & Nature Center

the essence of the Florida Keys

Nature lovers get a comfortable ride through Crane Point's scenic nature trail system.

Crane Point Museum

the trip

This is a fascinating and unique 63-acre site. It is home to the Museum of Natural History, Children's Activity Center, Adderley Town Historic Site and Marathon's Wild Bird Center. It includes an extensive nature trail system leading through a dense tropical forest to a spectacular view of Florida Bay.

what to see

Inside the museum, explore the history of the Keys. You will see a 600-year-old canoe crafted from a single log used by Key Indians in the 17th century and a Bellarmine jug from the 1500s, found in 1980 in near-perfect condition. You will also learn about Henry Flagler and his eight-year saga of building the Overseas Railroad from Miami to Key West. Completed in 1912, the railroad was destroyed by a powerful hurricane in 1935. You will see remnants of the railroad as you drive over the Seven Mile Bridge in Marathon, the longest in the Keys.

other highlights

A stop at the Children's Activity Center is a must for the kids. Here, they can climb aboard an interactive 17th-century galleon, "Los Niños de Los Cayos." Youngsters can also examine sea creatures in "touch tanks." To absorb the natural beauty of the Keys, walk along the boardwalk, part of the nearly three miles of nature trails.

Crane Point Museum & Nature Center
Mile Marker 50.5
5550 Overseas Highway (U.S. 1)
Marathon, FL 33050
(305) 743-9100

Admission: *$8 adults, $7 seniors 65 and older, $5 students up to 18, free for children 6 and younger.*

Hours: *Monday through Saturday 9 a.m. to 5 p.m., Sunday noon to 5 p.m.*

www.cranepoint.net

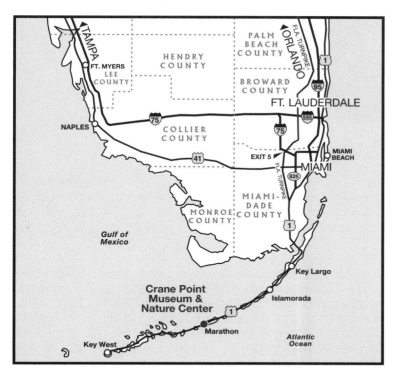

directions

From Tampa, take Interstate 75 south to exit 5 (Florida Turnpike south). Travel about 40 miles to the South Dixie Highway, which becomes U.S. 1 (Overseas Highway). Follow U.S. 1 about 75 miles to Crane Point Museum & Nature Center (Mile Marker 50.5).

a **chance** to see the **Keys** as they once **were.**

John Pennekamp Coral Reef State Park

the underwater spectacle in the Upper Keys

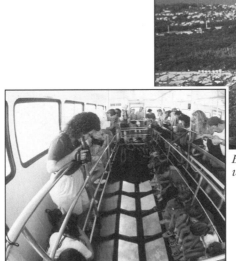

John Pennekamp State Park

Explore the magic of the underwater world.

the trip

John Pennekamp Coral Reef State Park is America's first underwater park. Scuba diving or snorkeling offers a unique opportunity to explore all the magic this amazing underwater world has to offer. You will see everything from incredible coral formations to vibrant, colorful fish.

what to see

Formed in the 1960s, Pennekamp Park encompasses more than 100-square miles of mangrove shoreline, grass flats and coral reef. Adjacent to Pennekamp is the Key Largo National Marine Sanctuary. Both of these pristine coral reef areas are protected by law against environmental abuse, assuring the preservation of this beautiful resource. If diving is not your thing, try snorkeling. They've got all the gear you need right there! There's plenty for landlubbers, too. Log some beach time, walk along the mangrove trail, canoe, kayak or pitch a tent at one of 47 camping sites.

other highlights

Located underwater at Key Largo Dry Rocks Reef is the "Christ of the Deep," a nine-foot tall bronze statue symbolizing peace among mankind.

John Pennekamp Coral Reef State Park
Mile Marker 102.5
Overseas Highway (U.S. 1)
Key Largo, FL 33037
(305) 451-1202

Admission: *Tour, courses, boat and equipment rental prices vary.*

Hours: *Snorkeling tours depart daily at 9 a.m., noon and 3 p.m. Scuba courses begin at 9 a.m.*

www.pennekamppark.com

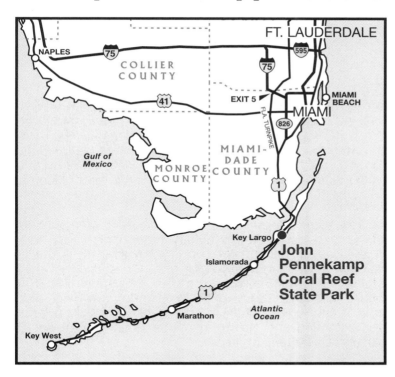

directions
From Tampa, take Interstate 75 south for about 250 miles to exit 5 (Florida Turnpike South). Travel about 40 miles to the South Dixie Highway, which becomes U.S. 1 (Overseas Highway). Travel south to Key Largo (Mile Marker 102.5).

world renowned for its dive and snorkeling attractions.

The Florida Keys & Key West

Key West at Daytime

a place for Parrot Heads

J. LaFray

Key West, a great place to party or simply enjoy the fabulous views, such as the Southernmost House, a gorgeous Victorian, that is a Key West landmark.

the trip

Key West is about so many things. And that includes getting from here to there...in no hurry. Just about anything and everything seems to take place on this Key, which is the southernmost tip of the United States. The days, however, are somewhat more subdued compared to the wild party nights. Take in all the fun of Duval Street, or simply cruise the network of historic streets teeming with interesting architecture, rich foliage and brilliant blooms.

what to see

On Duval Street, get your "cheeseburger in paradise" at Margaritaville owned by Florida singing legend Jimmy Buffett. Next door is Fast Buck Freddie's, Key West's incredible department store. If you feel like rockin', head over to Sloppy Joe's for a rollicking happy hour, or to the legendary Green Parrot (601 Whitehead St.) where folks have gathered for more than 100 years. If you want to kick back, relax and enjoy a sumptuous meal, Blue Heaven on Thomas Street (roosters et all) is a delectable choice. Its colorful history includes cockfighting and gambling. Other great choices are El Siboney for Cuban and La Trattoria for Italian.

other highlights

Enjoy a tour of the Hemingway House, where the famous author wrote many of his novels. Check out the six-toed cats; they are everywhere! For something off-the-beaten track, take the Key West Cemetery Tour and discover who's behind (and under) the raised coffins and quirky tombstone inscriptions. Bring home some Famous Florida® Key West Key lime juice from the Conch Tour Train Gift Shop where you can also purchase tickets for a comprehensive train tour of Key West.

Key West Chamber of Commerce
402 Wall Street
Key West, FL 33040
(305) 294-2587

Admission: *Free. Museum and tour rates vary.*

Hours: *Restaurant, shop and museum hours vary.*

www.keywestchamber.org

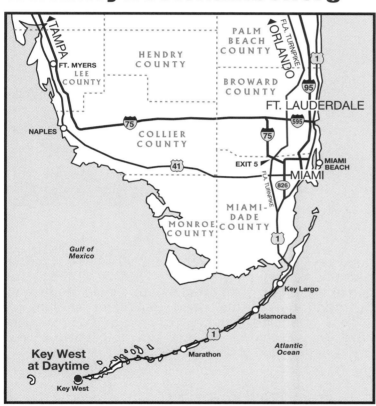

directions

From Tampa, take Interstate 75 south for about 250 miles to exit 5 (Florida Turnpike south). Travel about 40 miles to the South Dixie Highway, which becomes U.S. 1 (Overseas Highway). Follow U.S. 1 for about 120 miles to Key West. Turn right onto North Roosevelt Boulevard which becomes Truman Avenue. Follow Truman Avenue, then turn right onto Duval Street. Take Duval to Front Street, which overlooks Key West Harbor.

there's no **place** like it in the **world.**

Key West
Sunset Celebration

an evening fun fest

You'll get caught up in the carnival atmosphere in Key West.

Stuart Newman Associates

the trip

Many noted figures have enjoyed the sunset from Mallory Square over the years (Audubon wrote about it in the early 1800s). But the actual celebration began in the 1960s when carefree souls would go there to "watch Atlantis arising out of the cloud formations at sunset." Nowadays, musicians, artists, jugglers, clowns, psychics, food vendors and tourists gather every evening in Mallory Square to celebrate the close of another day in the tropical paradise known as Key West.

what to see

The celebration is an incubator for the arts and a launching pad for visual and performing art careers. Talented performers such as Dominique the Catman and tightrope walker Will Soto have been amazing folks at Key West sunsets for more than 20 years. Witness the Great Rondini's mind-boggling escape from chains and a strait jacket.

other highlights

Not to be overlooked are the countless arts and crafts exhibitors and food vendors. Feast your eyes on everything from jewelry to body art while gobbling down moist conch fritters, spicy Jamaican meat patties, fresh fruit smoothies and other gastronomic delights.

Mallory Square
Key West, FL 33040

Cultural Preservation Society
P.O. Box 4837
Key West, FL 33041
(305) 292-7700

Admission: *Free.*

Hours: *The Sunset Celebration begins 1 ½ hours before sunset every night.*

www.sunsetcelebration.org

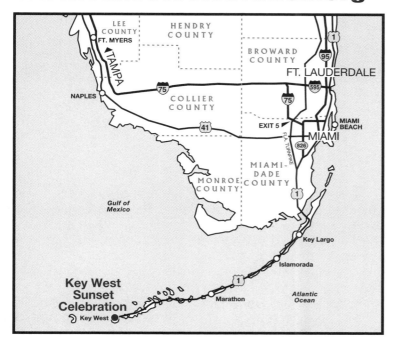

LEE COUNTY
HENDRY COUNTY
FT. MYERS
TAMPA
BROWARD COUNTY
FT. LAUDERDALE
75
NAPLES
COLLIER COUNTY
595
75
EXIT 5
MIAMI BEACH
41
FLA. TURNPIKE
MIAMI
826
MIAMI-DADE COUNTY
MONROE COUNTY
1
Gulf of Mexico
Key Largo
Islamorada
Key West Sunset Celebration
Key West
Marathon
Atlantic Ocean
1

directions
From Tampa, take Interstate 75 south for about 250 miles to exit 5 (Florida Turnpike south). Travel about 40 miles to the South Dixie Highway, which becomes U.S. 1 (Overseas Highway). Follow U.S. 1 for about 120 miles to Key West. Turn right onto North Roosevelt Boulevard which becomes Truman Avenue. Follow Truman Avenue, then turn right onto Duval Street. Take Duval to the end, make a left onto Wall Street into the parking lot. Walk towards sunset.

there **is** more **than** a **bit** of a **carnival** atmosphere, and **you'll** probably get **caught** up in all of **it.**

The Florida Keys & Key West

Nautilimo

all at sea with memories

Nautilimo

*Yes, heads turn when this seagoing luxury car sails by.
Called Nautilimo, it is a unique way to cruise.*

the trip

Tour the Keys in the world's first Cadillac-style, nautical stretch Limousine. This one-of-a-kind transport can accommodate 1 to 6 passengers on a leisurely cruise along the sheltered waters of Florida Bay. It's an especially nice ride at sunset. And like the Nautilimo itself, owner Joe Fox is a one-of-a-kind.

what to see

Joe built his Nautilimo by hand and here's how he did it: he created a 1987 Cadillac replica out of fiberglass and mounted it all on a Carolina skiff. Then he added a custom Yamaha, four-stroke, 100-horsepower engine. Several accessory trips to the junkyard later and his dream had come true!

other highlights

Up to four people can take a short jaunt or a two-hour trip with music and champagne. It's available for birthdays, anniversaries, weddings or a romantic sunset cruise for two. This crazy contraption just makes everyone feel good! You will love the reaction from onlookers as Joe passes by waterfront restaurants and the like.

Nautilimo
Lorelei Restaurant & Marina
Mile Marker 82 Bayside
Islamorada, FL 33060
(305) 942-3793

Admission: *Two-hour tour $110. Rates may vary.*

Hours: *Tour times vary. Call for reservations.*

www.nautilimo.com

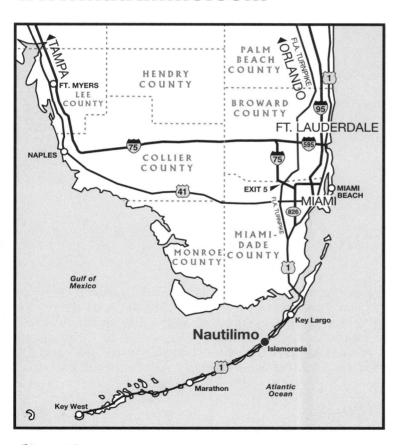

directions
From Tampa, take Interstate 75 south for about 250 miles to exit 5 (Florida Turnpike south). Travel about 40 miles to the South Dixie Highway, which becomes U.S. 1 (Overseas Highway). Follow U.S. 1 to Dogwood Lane. (Mile Marker 82). Turn left into the marina.

a **Caddy** for the **Keys.**

Robbie's of Islamorada

feed the tarpon!

Robbie's of Islamorada

Grab some bait fish and feed lunch to the schools of hungry tarpon that make Robbie's their home.

the trip

Here in the sportfishing capital of the world, feeding fish is more fun than catching them.

what to see

Robbie's is best known for "feeding the tarpon." For obvious reasons, these savvy fish have decided to call this place home. It all began 32 years ago with the feeding of an injured fish named "Scarface." Today, it's an amazing spectacle: hand-feeding schools of 50 to 100 tarpon. These big guys actually jump out of the water and take the food right out of your hand! For a few dollars and a bit of courage, you can do it too!

other highlights

From here you can embark on one of the most popular Robbie's tours, rent a kayak or go on a jet ski tour, hire a back country or patch reef fishing guide, or rent a boat and chart your own course. Type "A" personalities take care – this place exudes a laid-back atmosphere. You're likely to find yourself in a rocking chair on the palm frond-covered deck sipping a cold beverage and discussing tides, favorite fishing holes or even politics with one of the old timers who hang out there.

Robbie's Of Islamorada
77522 Overseas Highway (U.S. 1)
Mile Marker 77.5
Islamorada, FL 33036
(305) 664-9814
Toll free: (877) 664-8498

Admission: *Fishing and tour rates vary. Tarpon feeding $1, plus $2.79 for a pail of bait fish.*

Hours: *Daily 8 a.m. to 8 p.m. Call to confirm times.*

www.robbies.com

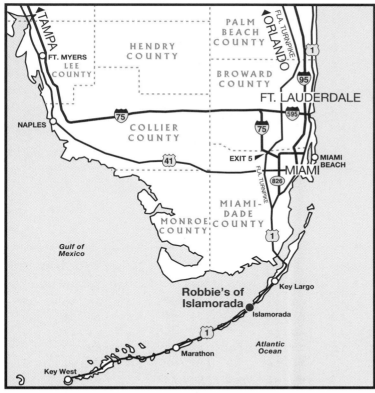

Tarpon feeding **is** the local **Sport!**

directions

From Tampa, take Interstate 75 south for about 250 miles to exit 5 (Florida Turnpike south). Travel about 40 miles to the South DIxie Highway, which becomes U.S. 1 (Overseas Highway). Follow U.S. 1 about 40 miles to Robbie's of Islamorada. (Mile Marker 77.5).

weather guide

FOX 13 WEATHER
TM FOX

	Fort Myers		Jacksonville		Key West		Miami	
	High/Low	Rainfall	High/Low	Rainfall	High/Low	Rainfall	High/Low	Rainfall
January	74°/53°	1.8"	64°/42°	3.3"	75°/65°	2.0"	75°/59°	2.0"
February	76°/54°	2.2"	67°/44°	3.9"	75°/65°	1.8"	76°/60°	2.1"
March	80°/59°	3.1"	74°/50°	3.7"	79°/69°	1.7"	79°/64°	2.4"
April	85°/62°	1.1"	80°/56°	2.8"	82°/72°	1.8"	83°/68°	3.0"
May	89°/68°	3.9"	85°/63°	3.6"	85°/76°	3.5"	85°/72°	6.2"
June	91°/73°	9.5"	89°/70°	5.7"	88°/79°	5.1"	88°/75°	9.3"
July	91°/75°	8.3"	92°/73°	5.6"	89°/80°	3.6"	89°/77°	5.7"
August	91°/75°	9.7"	91°/72°	7.9"	89°/79°	5.0"	89°/77°	7.6"
September	90°/74°	7.8"	87°/70°	7.1"	88°/79°	5.9"	88°/76°	7.6"
October	86°/69°	2.9"	80°/60°	2.9"	84°/76°	4.4"	85°/72°	5.6"
November	81°/61°	1.6"	73°/50°	2.2"	80°/71°	2.8"	80°/67°	2.7"
December	76°/55°	1.6"	67°/44°	2.7"	76°/67°	2.0"	77°/62°	1.8"

	Orlando		Pensacola		Tampa Bay		Tallahassee	
	High/Low	Rainfall	High/Low	Rainfall	High/Low	Rainfall	High/Low	Rainfall
January	72°/51°	2.3"	60°/41°	4.7"	70°/49°	2.0"	63°/38°	4.8"
February	72°/50°	4.0"	63°/44°	5.4"	71°/51°	3.1"	66°/40°	5.5"
March	78°/56°	3.2"	69°/51°	5.7"	77°/56°	3.0"	73°/47°	6.2"
April	84°/61°	1.3"	76°/58°	3.4"	82°/61°	1.2"	80°/52°	3.7"
May	88°/67°	3.1"	83°/66°	4.2"	87°/67°	3.1"	86°/61°	4.8"
June	91°/72°	7.5"	89°/72°	6.4"	90°/73°	5.5"	91°/68°	6.9"
July	92°/74°	7.2"	90°/74°	7.4"	90°/74°	6.6"	91°/71°	8.8"
August	91°/74°	7.1"	89°/74°	7.3"	90°/74°	7.6"	91°/71°	7.5"
September	89°/73°	6.3"	86°/70°	5.4"	89°/73°	6.0"	88°/68°	5.6"
October	84°/67°	2.9"	79°/60°	4.1"	84°/65°	2.0"	81°/56°	2.9"
November	77°/57°	1.7"	70°/51°	3.5"	78°/57°	1.8"	73°/46°	3.9"
December	73°/52°	2.0"	63°/44°	4.3"	72°/52°	2.2"	66°/41°	5.0"

One Tank Trips®: Hidden Treasures

about Florida weather

As you make your plans to travel around Florida using **One Tank Trips®: The Hidden Treasures,** I thought you would like to know the average high and low temperatures and rainfall. For your convenience, I have prepared the accompanying chart to use as a reference.

For the most part, Florida weather is typically pleasant. In the summer, afternoon rains are almost a daily occurrence. But please be aware that there is always the possibility of dangerous lightning, tornadoes, floods and even hurricanes. Hurricane season begins in June and runs through the end of November. If a hurricane is approaching, I urge you to take watches and warnings seriously.

For the latest weather updates and information log onto **www.myfoxtampabay.com** where you will find SkyTower OMNI radar views along with our hurricane and severe weather guide. You can also use your mobile phone/PDA to see the latest SkyTower OMNI radar views. For additional hurricane information, log onto **www.myfoxhurricane.com**.

Here's wishing you lots of smiles and laughter and, above all, enjoy your travels!

Paul Dellegatto
WTVT FOX13 Chief Meteorologist

about Florida Sports

In the Bay Area, you can cheer on our college and pro sports teams at some of the finest stadium facilities in the country. The University of South Florida has broken into the big time when it comes to NCAA football and Tampa is also the home of the ACC Championship game and the Outback Bowl.

"Fire the cannons!" The Tampa Bay Buccaneers and their famous pirate ship are a must see for the adventurous football fan. You can also cool your heels when the Tampa Bay Lightning heat up the ice or you could take a swing at Major League Baseball when the Tampa Bay Rays take the field in St. Petersburg. If you have a need for speed, you're just a tankful away from the biggest race in motor sports, the Daytona 500.

So, pick a sport, pick a spot to travel to, then pile the family in the car and enjoy a **One Tank Trip**® to some of the best athletic events in America.

Chip Carter
WTVT FOX 13 Sports Director

SUNSHINE STATE SPORTS ATTRACTIONS

Major League Baseball – www.mlb.com
Florida Marlins, Dolphin Stadium, Miami
Tampa Bay Rays, Tropicana Field, St. Petersburg

Spring Training Baseball (Grapefruit League)
Atlanta Braves, Disney's Wide World of Sports, Kissimmee
Baltimore Orioles, Fort Lauderdale Stadium, Fort Lauderdale
Boston Red Sox, City of Palms Park, Fort Myers
Cincinnati Reds, Ed Smith Stadium, Sarasota
Cleveland Indians, Chain of Lakes Park, Winter Haven
Detroit Tigers, Joker Marchant Stadium, Lakeland
Florida Marlins, Roger Deam Stadium, Jupiter

Houston Astros, Osceola County Stadium, Kissimmee
Los Angeles Dodgers, Holman Stadium, Vero Beach
New York Mets, Tradition Field, Port St. Lucie
New York Yankees, Legends Field, Tampa
Philadelphia Phillies, Bright House Networks Field, Clearwater
Pittsburgh Pirates, McKechnie Field, Bradenton
Tampa Bay Rays, Charlotte Sports Park, Port Charlotte
Toronto Blue Jays, Knology Park, Dunedin

National Basketball Association – www.nba.com
Orlando Magic, Orlando Arena, Orlando
Miami Heat, American Airlines Arena, Miami

National Football League – www.nfl.com
Tampa Bay Buccaneers, Raymond James Stadium, Tampa
Jacksonville Jaguars, Alltel Stadium, Jacksonville
Miami Dolphins, Dolphin Stadium, Miami

Arena Football League – www.arenafootball.com
Tampa Bay Storm, St. Pete Times Forum, Tampa
Orlando Predators, Orlando Arena, Orlando

National Hockey League – www.nhl.com
Tampa Bay Lightning, St. Pete Times Forum, Tampa
Florida Panthers, National Car Rental Center, Miami

NASCAR and International Racing – www.nascar.com
Daytona International Speedway, Daytona Beach
Homestead-Miami Speedway, Homestead
USA International Speedway, Lakeland
Sebring International Raceway, Sebring

College Athletics
Bethune-Cookman University, Daytona Beach
Florida A&M University, Tallahassee
Florida State University, Tallahassee
University of Florida, Gainesville
University of Central Florida, Orlando
University of Miami, Coral Gables
University of South Florida, Tampa

i n d e x

X-Y-Z